**Religious Responses to Modernity**

# Workshops on Religion

The Israel Academy of Sciences and Humanities
Berlin-Brandenburgische Akademie der Wissenschaften

# Religious Responses to Modernity

Edited by Yohanan Friedmann
and Christoph Markschies

berlin-brandenburgische
AKADEMIE DER WISSENSCHAFTEN

DE GRUYTER

האקדמיה הלאומית הישראלית למדעים
المجمع الوطني الإسرائيلي للعلوم والآداب
THE ISRAEL ACADEMY OF SCIENCES AND HUMANITIES

ISBN 978-3-11-112073-7
e-ISBN (PDF) 978-3-11-072398-4
e-ISBN (EPUB) 978-3-11-072406-6

**Library of Congress Control Number: 2020952294**

**Bibliographic information published by the Deutsche Nationalbibliothek**
The Deutsche Nationalbibliothek lists this publication in the Deutsche Nationalbibliografie; detailed bibliographic data are available on the Internet at http://dnb.dnb.de.


This volume is text- and page-identical with the hardback published in 2021.
Cover image: The mausoleum of Immanuel Kant (1724–1804) at Immanuel Kant State University of Russia, Kaliningrad. The structure, designed by Friedrich Lahrs, was erected in 1924, marking the bicentenary of Kant's birth. iStock.com/leonkenig.
Printing and binding: CPI books GmbH, Leck

www.degruyter.com

# Table of Contents

Foreword *by Christoph Markschies* —— **VII**

Simon Gerber
**The Rise and Decline of Protestant Rationalism —— 1**

Johannes Zachhuber
**Individual and Community in Modern Debates about Religion and Secularism —— 11**

Jonathan Garb
**The Conversion of the Jews: Identity as Ontology in Modern Kabbalah —— 33**

Rivka Feldhay
**Catholic Europe and Sixteenth-Century Science: A Path to Modernity? —— 49**

Paul Mendes-Flohr
**Jewish Intellectuals on the Chimera of Progress: Walter Benjamin, Martin Buber and Leo Strauss —— 64**

Israel Gershoni
**Depoliticization and Denationalization of Religion: Aḥmad Luṭfī al-Sayyid and the Relocation of Islam in Modern Life —— 79**

Christoph Schmidt
**Socrates against Christ? A Theological Critique of Michel Foucault's Philosophy of Parrhesia —— 113**

Contributors to This Volume —— **135**

Index
- Places and Institutions —— **137**
- Names —— **139**

# Foreword

The cathedral of Kaliningrad, erected in the fourteenth century and carefully rebuilt after suffering severe destruction in World War II, stands in the middle of the city on a small, landscaped piece of land. It is a Gothic cathedral with a strongly fortified character. East Prussia was always a border region and also occasionally an exclave, as part of either the German state or the Russian Empire. The church's sanctuary contains a hall that was built of porphyry in 1924. It attracts a great number of visitors, which no doubt rescued the cathedral from complete demolition after 1945.

This structure holds the cenotaph of the philosopher Immanuel Kant, erected there on the two hundredth anniversary of his birth, because the old professors' crypt of the nearby university had become dilapidated. Nowadays, if you should visit the Immanuel Kant Baltic Federal University in Kaliningrad as part of an official delegation, you will be taken to the grave to lay a carnation there. Kant is not buried inside the cathedral, because the professors of Albertina University, as it was called until 1945, were buried in the professors' crypt, adjoining the church building. Indeed, a story already in circulation in the nineteenth century fits well with this location: At official university celebrations, which had the character of a church service, Kant, it is said, always stepped out of the procession of professors and did not enter the cathedral. Nevertheless, whether Kant's grave should be relocated into the church has been a subject of recurrent debates, and his academic funeral service took place in the cathedral.

In front of the cathedral, on the other side of the sanctuary from Kant's grave, is a lesser-known stone commemorating the theologian Friedrich Julius Leopold Rupp (1809–1884), a private lecturer at the university and a participant in the Friends of the Light movement, who set up a free Protestant congregation in Königsberg. The relief medallion on the memorial stone, situated where his house once stood, is one of the earliest works of Käthe Kollwitz.

Kant, the Friends of the Light and Königsberg – when examining the topic of "Religious Responses to Modernity," one must, from the perspective of the Christian religion, speak of Königsberg. The royal, commercial and university city, steeped in tradition and located in what is now Russian territory, stands paradigmatically for various attempts to modernize the Christian religion. Albert, Duke of Prussia, after whom the University was first named, modernized the religious Prussian State of the Teutonic Order, dating back to the time of the Crusades, and turned it into a "modern" secular duchy under Polish suzerainty. He also created educational institutions that aimed to serve the "modernization" of his religion. Kant discussed religion within the boundaries of reason, and Rupp, along with

https://doi.org/10.1515/9783110723984-203

like-minded colleagues, created a Free Protestant Congregation outside of the Prussian national church, because he no longer believed that Prussia's Protestant state church was capable of modernizing. All of these interconnected matters are dealt with herein by Simon Gerber.

One could also discuss the connections between religion, politics and secularization in the development of the Königsberg region, from its time under the rule of the State of the Teutonic Order to its becoming a province of the social-democratically governed state of Prussia in the Weimar Republic. In this volume, however, Johannes Zachhuber embarks on a wider exploration of the roots of theory formation within these contexts and their beginnings in antiquity. Above all, he points out that the topic cannot be examined without a careful analysis of individuality and individualization. He further includes in the discussion an element of the conservative discourse around modernization from a nineteenth-century French Roman Catholic perspective.

The modern, and therefore modernization, are hardly monolithic. It has become increasingly clear, as expressed by Shmuel Eisenstadt via his now-classic concept of "multiple modernities," that the Central European narrative of a gradual modernization of the Christian religion and its relationship to politics and society, in the form of rationalization and secularization, neither adequately describes the situation in Europe, nor can it be applied globally. Indeed, that is why the Berlin-Brandenburg Academy of Sciences and the Israel Academy of the Sciences and Humanities established their joint comparative project on the rationalization of religions, with the intention of juxtaposing the Christianity of central Europe, influenced as it was by Protestantism, with the various currents that transpired in Judaism and Islam as well.

In this volume, Jonathan Garb examines different currents in the Kabbala, demonstrating that very different cities, such as Prague and New York, can, like Königsberg, be viewed as paradigmatic backdrops for the interrelations between religions, modernities and modernization processes. At the same time, it becomes clear that not only globalization and the transcending of national borders, but also nationalization processes must be understood as integral to some forms of modernization.

Rivka Feldhay, with her outline of an archaeology of the knowledge–religion–state configuration in Catholic Europe between around 1550 and 1650, again demonstrates the fruitfulness of Eisenstadt's paradigm of "multiple modernities" in coloring the picture of Europe's early modern history and the "confessionalization" process described by Heinz Schilling.

Paul Mendes-Flohr demonstrates that criticism of the modern can also be counted among the "multiple modernities." References to the ambivalences of the modern, such as those of Walter Benjamin or Martin Buber, may hinder theories, and even society as a whole, from settling down comfortably into their respective modernities, thus implicitly bringing the dynamics of modernization more or less to a halt. It is then, specifically, that the critique of modernism actually proves itself an instrument of modernization.

Israel Gershoni's chapter in this volume makes the singular contribution of breaking up monolithic views of Islam, by showing how the Egyptian intellectual and historian Luṭfī al-Sayyid campaigned for the depoliticization and denationalization of religion. Bringing a global and comparative perspective to a given subject makes it possible to involve authors and theories from very different times and contexts in the discussion, which is what Christoph Schmidt achieves in his chapter on Foucault's philosophy of Parrhesia.

At first glance, it seems almost trivial to say that different religions, and the various currents within them, have reacted in very different ways to "multiple modernities," but things become more interesting when the comparative perspective leads us to discover surprising similarities. Disparate encounters are connected by their transnational or national perspectives, with the one side criticizing in the interest of rationality as a model of authorization, and the other presenting revelation as a critique of a depraved form of rationality. However, care must be exercised to ensure that the theorem of "multiple modernities," which allows for such interesting comparative studies, does not lead to a democratic and open society becoming quasi-indifferent to the effects of certain hostile movements when making comparisons of this kind. The contents of this volume show, by contrast, that criticism of totalitarianisms acting in the name of rationality and modernity is also possible from the heart of a religious worldview. By providing a counterweight to the popularity of some all-too-simplified models of modernization, I believe the volume has already fulfilled an important function.

The Israel Academy of Sciences and Humanities was an excellent host to the conference from which this volume emerged, and it was a pleasure to prepare the encounter and edit the volume together with Yohanan Friedmann. Deborah Greniman of the Academy's Publications Department invested a great deal of work in copy-editing and preparing the volume as a joint publication of our two Academies with De Gruyter. Finally, thanks go to Sophie Wagenhofer and Alice Meroz at De Gruyter for their kind support of the series generated by our joint conferences and their efforts to ensure the production of a handsome finished product.

*Christoph Markschies, Berlin-Brandenburgische Akademie der Wissenschaften*
*Berlin, Summer 2020*

Simon Gerber

# The Rise and Decline of Protestant Rationalism

## Kant on Revealed and Natural Religion

> *Religion* is (subjectively considered) the recognition of all our duties as divine commands. That religion, in which I must first know that something is a divine command in order that I recognize it as my duty, is *revealed* religion (or a religion which requires a revelation); by contrast, that religion in which I must first know that something is duty before I can acknowledge it as a divine command is *natural religion*.[1]

Thus wrote Immanuel Kant in his treatise on religion within the boundaries of mere reason. Religion, according to Kant, is the means to help humanity unite in a universal ethical community; but to constitute such an ethical community, as a Kingdom of God, religion must be public, and the community must take shape in the form of a visible church founded by human beings on statutory laws. For a religion underlying such a universal church, no knowledge based on an assertoric dogmatic belief is required – a knowledge that must remain hypothetical. The recognition of ethical duties that can claim general acknowledgement as divine commandments, and the consequences of that recognition for the idea of God, are the only basis for a universal church. A visible church with its statutory laws that claims to be true and universal must have the principle of coming closer and closer to the pure religion of reason. If a duty is but recognized because of its revelation as a divine commandment, the religion is a revealed religion that must be instructed and learned, but if I recognize a duty as a general one by myself and conclude therefrom its divine importance, the religion is a natural or rational one.[2]

Now:

> Anyone who declares natural religion as alone morally necessary, i.e. a duty, can also be called *rationalist* (in matters of faith). If he denies the reality of any supernatural divine revelation, he is called *naturalist*; should he, however, allow this revelation, yet claim that to take cognizance of it and accept it as actual is not necessarily required for religion, then he can be named *pure rationalist*; but, if he holds that faith in divine revelation is necessary to universal religion, then he can be called pure *supernaturalist* in matters of faith.[3]

---

**1** Kant 1996:177. Emphasis in the original (1794:229–230).

**2** Kant 1794:225–231 (1907:151–154; 1996:175–177).

**3** Kant 1996:177–178. Emphasis in the original (1794:231–232).

https://doi.org/10.1515/9783110723984-001

It is obvious that Kant prefers the rationalist's position, but he does not regard the difference as a strict opposition: The rationalist will not claim to prove the impossibility of divine revelation, and a religion can be natural and revealed, if revelation helps to obtain it though it ought and could have been invented by use of reason.[4] So Christianity is both a revealed religion taught by the teacher Jesus and a doctrine in agreement with pure rational faith.[5]

## Neology, Rationalism and Supernaturalism

The enlightened neologists or neologs of the eighteenth century had already endeavored to make Protestant doctrine simpler, more popular, more modern and more evident: Christian religion is in harmony with natural innate ideas about God and virtue, but Christianity and Christian ministry are more capable than natural reason and virtue of comforting, of strengthening human honesty and of advancing worldly and eternal bliss.[6] The final stages of Protestant Enlightenment theology followed Kant and have been called, respectively, rationalism and supernaturalism;[7] the conflict between these two directions arose in the early nineteenth century.

Rationalism agreed with neology in striving for rational evidence, simplicity, practicability and popular education. But it had learned from Kant that any knowledge about supersensible realities or divine beings cannot be attained by means of theoretical reason. Rationalism stressed that the use of one's own reason instead of following foreign authorities is the first duty of all autonomous rational beings.

Supernaturalism, too, referred to Kant: If human reason is not able to form certain judgements about transcendental realities, then supernatural revelation is required to make us sure about everything that pure reason postulates in order to found moral law: the existence of God, divine providence, the order of salvation and the final judgement. So faith cannot renounce Holy Scripture; it takes therefrom all the knowledge that it needs from beyond the boundary of pure reason.[8]

4 Kant 1794:231–235 (1907:154–157; 1996:177–179).
5 Kant 1794:235–246 (1907:157–167; 1996:179–188).
6 Cf. Aner 1929:esp. 61–143; Beutel 2009:112–151, 221–222.
7 Cf. Reinhard 1810:95; Hahn 1827:21–25.
8 Cf. Rohls 1997:297–308, 389–393; Beutel 2009:160–169.

Though rationalism is the last shape in which Enlightenment theology occurs, it postdates the first attempts to overcome Enlightenment. In 1799, the young Reformed hospital chaplain Friedrich Schleiermacher wrote in his Speeches on Religion:

> Religion's essence is neither thinking nor acting, but intuition and feeling. [...] Praxis is an art, speculation is a science, religion is sensibility and taste for the infinite.[9]

> So-called natural religion is usually so refined and has such philosophical and moral manners that it allows little of the unique character of religion to shine through.[10]

Schleiermacher contradicted the enlightened ideal of natural and rational religion, the utility of religion for the common life, and the contamination of religion with morals and metaphysics. Religion is not obliged to be useful for any purpose beside itself. It is a kind of intuiting the world and everything in the world as one universe – an artistic Weltanschauung rather than a scientific one.

Friedrich Wilhelm Joseph Schelling, too, in his lectures on academic studies, settled accounts with Enlightenment theology: While the object of philosophy is the original knowledge, the supreme identity and indifference of spirit and nature, of intelligence and reality, Christian religion means to interpret the universe as an allegory of this supreme identity and indifference, as the absolute realizing itself in history, as the reconciliation of nature, necessity and freedom, as God realizing himself in history, as God made man. The ecclesiastical dogmas try to find phrases for this speculative truth; they represent an advance in comparison with the earlier documents of Christianity, like the New Testament. Modern Enlightenment theology, Schelling wrote, wanted to clarify Christian religion, but instead it cleared religion out. It had neither understanding nor appreciation for the idea; it wanted to explain everything according to morals and according to empiricism, and in so doing it lost the main thing, the speculative idea; it meant shallowness triumphing over profundity.[11]

Rationalism stood not only against the old literal orthodoxy, Pietism and Biblicism, and against supernaturalism; it also stood against new pantheistic and idealistic ideas, that is, against transgressing the boundaries drawn by Kant against all speculation on sublime matters.

---

**9** [Schleiermacher] 1799:50, 52–53 (1984:211–212; 1996:22–23).
**10** [Schleiermacher] 1799:243 (1984:296; 1996:98).
**11** Schelling 1803:151–210 (1859:279–305).

## Wegscheider's *Institutiones*

In 1815, a new dogmatic textbook appeared under the title *Institutiones theologiae Christianae dogmaticae* – Instruction of Christian dogmatic theology. Its author, Julius Wegscheider, born in 1771 in the Duchy of Brunswick, was a disciple of the prominent rationalist Konrad Henke at Helmstedt. In 1804, Wegscheider had defended Kant's doctrine of religion against "the separation of morals from religion postulated by recent philosophy"[12] – that is, by Schleiermacher and romanticism. Since 1810 Wegscheider had been a professor at Halle. His lectures were reputed to be dry but clear, distinct and instructive, and they attracted hundreds of students.[13]

This combination of dryness and clarity characterizes not only Wegscheider's lectures, but also his textbook on dogmatics. It is divided into an introduction called *Prolegomena* and three main parts, concerning Holy Scripture, God and Humanity. The *Prolegomena* establish the rationalistic standpoint: Concerning divine matters, reason is to be used not only as the formal principle but also as the material one.[14] Not to use reason would deny it and would offend human dignity; authority and sensual perception without reason can neither give certainty nor claim general recognition. Both piety and moral respectability are based on reason and closely connected by reason.[15] Wegscheider does not deny revelation, but any revelation is natural and accords with God's providential work in nature, which does not skip the natural causal connections. With the increasing of rational insight, revelation and external authority must recede.[16]

The sections of the main parts offer a clear and logical compilation of everything relevant to the problem under discussion, from the Old and New Testaments, through the Church Fathers, medieval authors, reformers and Protestant symbols, up to modern authors. The concluding *Epicrisis* summarizes the argument in a way that both corresponds to the testimony of Scripture and satisfies the claims of rational insight.

Reason, according to Wegscheider, is the organon that facilitates critique and appreciation of the biblical, dogmatic and ecclesiastical traditions, and distinction between the true core and the veil of older mythological or superstitious conceptions that obscures it. Supernatural causes or immediate divine intervention

12 Wegscheider 1804.
13 Hoffmann 1908:35.
14 Wegscheider 1833:49 (§11)
15 *Ibid.*, x (Praefatio), 15–16 (§3), 50–51 (§11)
16 *Ibid.*, xiv–xv (Praefatio), 51-53 (§11), 58–60 (§12)

cannot be acknowledged; what is traditionally derived therefrom must be explained as a product of accommodation or of defective knowledge of natural occurrences.[17] The Bible itself is not a uniform work; it exhibits developing views and different types of doctrine, and many things have been distorted and warped over the course of centuries of exegesis. Wegscheider knows all that and takes it into consideration, and you cannot maintain that he is a bad exegete who interprets the texts at will.

Wegscheider appreciated the traditional proofs of God's existence: Although they did not actually prove God's existence, they showed that atheism is absurd.[18] The divine trinity manifested God's singularity; the unique dignity of Christ, who as teacher of the truth, was the envoy and instrument of divine providence; and God's efficacy in preserving human liberty.[19] Justification by faith meant gaining God's pleasure by means of a well-disposed mind, rather than by individual meritorious deeds.[20] The likelihood of the soul's immortality was attested by consensus of most of the nations and by arguments of theoretical and practical philosophy.[21]

Wegscheider's *Institutiones* was a highly successful textbook. Nowadays, other contemporaneous books in the field are more renowned, especially Schleiermacher's *Glaubenslehre* (1821–1822),[22] but also Philipp Marheineke's *Grundlehren der christlichen Dogmatik* (1819),[23] the latter influenced by Schelling and Hegel. Yet, while the dogmatics of Schleiermacher and Marheineke each went through two editions in the decade after their respective publications, Wegscheider's went through seven between 1815 and 1833 (an eighth edition was published in 1844). And no wonder: Wegscheider's book was neither original nor ingenious nor innovative, but readers of Latin can nevertheless still learn much from its rich trove of information on religious controversies and its collection of *dicta probantia* on every theme, from the Bible to modern times. Innumerable rural and small-town clergymen owned it and consulted it on all questions relating to faith and preaching.[24] Among early nineteenth-century theologians, wrote Karl Barth, Wegscheider was the "philistine bourgeois."[25]

---

**17** *Ibid.*:61 (§12), 117–119 (§26)
**18** *Ibid.*:238 (§57)
**19** *Ibid.*:337–338 (§93)
**20** *Ibid.*:542–543 (§155)
**21** *Ibid.*:671–672 (§194)
**22** Schleiermacher 1830–1831 [1821–1822].
**23** Marheineke 1827 [1819].
**24** Cf. Barth 1952:423.
**25** *Ibid.*:427, 432.

Clearly, after all, rationalism is to an extent a conservative rather than a progressive movement. Like the old orthodoxy, it regarded the clergy as the elementary educators of the people and the consistories of the State Church as the executive organs of a wise government (provided that rationalism was in power), whereas all fashionable ideas about religious friendship were but mystical enthusiasm. For example, Henke, Wegscheider's teacher, was not only a critical church historian and a rational dogmatist at the university; he also held a high office in the official Lutheran Church of the Duchy of Brunswick.

## Hase versus Röhr

In 1830, Ernst Wilhelm Hengstenberg's conservative *Evangelische Kirchenzeitung* launched an attack against the rationalist professors at Halle, Wegscheider and Wilhelm Gesenius: These two opposed as erroneous what the evangelical church by its confessions recognized as the truth. What should the students who were obliged to frequent their lessons do once they were in office? Should they preach what they had learnt to despise as superstitious, while trying to intersperse some of the typical moral trivialities that bored everybody? Gesenius, Wegscheider and many others protested against this denunciation. The Prussian King Frederick William III ordered a thorough inquiry, but the rationalists ultimately were acquitted.[26]

A few years later, however, rationalism suffered its decisive defeat. What happened? Karl August Hase, a young scholar at Jena, published a booklet on dogmatics entitled *Hutterus redivivus* – Hütter reborn. Though shorter, its form to an extent resembles that of Wegscheider's *Institutiones*: It is a relatively short text with long footnotes citing and discussing various opinions about theological questions. What was special about it is that Hase, himself a liberal Protestant influenced by Schelling, Schleiermacher and Hegel, sought to discuss these issues from the point of view of old Leonhard Hütter, or Hutterus, an early defender of Lutheran orthodoxy, who, over two centuries before, had published a popular compendium of *Loci theologici* according to the Bible and the symbols of the Lutheran Church. If Hütter were to come back to life, how would he now explain to us the classic doctrine of Protestantism, and how would he converse with modern schools of thought, like neology, idealism and rationalism?[27]

**26** Cf. Bachmann 1880:177–283; *ibid.*, Beilage, 21–60.

**27** Hase 1833:iii–vii.

Apart from Wegscheider, one of the most renowned rationalists was Johann Friedrich Röhr, who was not a professor at the university but a prominent church dignitary, the General Superintendent of the Duchy of Sachsen-Weimar-Eisenach; in 1832 he had delivered the eulogy for Goethe. According to Röhr's popular *Letters on Rationalism*, an epistolatory defense of rationalism, the purpose of the New Testament was to express the truths of rational religion.[28] Röhr responded to Hase's *Hutterus redivivus* in his review journal, the *Kritische Predigerbibliothek* (Critical Library of Preachers):

> What is this *Hutterus redivivus* to us? Who summoned up this shade of an evangelical scholastic from the tomb of the sixteenth century? What has he got to tell the sons of the nineteenth century? Would he vainly boast of making us forget what three centuries have gained in better insight into the spirit of the gospel and in better philosophical systematization of its content?

Röhr suspected Hase of introducing his Schellingian mystical phantasms under the guise of ecclesiastical orthodoxy.[29]

This review set off a dispute in which both sides collected their writings in anthologies, entitled, respectively, *Anti-Hasiana* and *Anti-Röhr*. The title *Anti-Röhr*, Hase wrote, recalled Lessing's *Anti-Goeze*, an anthology of polemics against the Hamburg pastor Melchior Goeze. The dispute between Lessing and Goeze, over biblical letter, spirit and freedom, had been a collision of two principles and two ages – scriptural orthodoxy and Enlightenment. The same was now the case with himself and Röhr: Two ages were colliding.[30]

Hase declared that the doctrine set out in his *Hutterus redivivus* was not his own view, and that one must be a little sophisticated to maintain an old orthodoxy in modern times; the *Hutterus redivivus* was to be understood as a historical exposition. Nevertheless, this old doctrine still had more strength and was greater and more consistent than most of the modern attempts. The main problem wasn't Schelling but rationalism, and while the latter had its role and its historical merit, the "vulgar rationalism" (as it was called in the theological review journal *Rheinwalds Repertorium*) of Röhr and Wegscheider lacked all understanding of history and religion. And what kind of reason was the touchstone by which Röhr sought to test and examine all things? It were neither science nor speculation, but merely ordinary common sense. With this, Röhr claimed to represent true Protestantism, but Christianity was neither founded on common sense nor

**28** Röhr 1813:129.
**29** [Röhr] 1836:1–2.
**30** Hase 1837:v–vi.

reformed by it in Luther's time. For itself, declared Hase, common sense was nothing but banality and triviality.[31]

## The Lichtfreunde

Rationalism's last step was a sometimes broad movement for freedom of dogmas and of spiritual tutelage, at a time when philosophy, *Weltanschauung*, epistemology and ethics were already pursuing routes that parted from rationalistic optimism.[32] In 1841, after a pastor was sensationally reprimanded for calling the prayer to Christ superstition, eight theologians met at Gnadau and founded an association for the preservation of all the attainments of Enlightenment within the broad church. In May 1845, two or three thousand people attended the ninth general assembly of the association at Köthen – the Protestant Friends, as they called themselves, or the Lichtfreunde, Friends of the Light, as they were called by the people, theologians and laity, especially primary school teachers. They acknowledged as true and corresponding to their principles the maxim that the living spirit dwelling within, and not the biblical letter, was the true rule for the free Protestant consciousness.

This was followed by conflicts with state and church authorities and the founding of free religious congregations, which were granted full liberty in 1858. In the following decades, however, first the Christian content and then the congregations themselves thinned out and mostly vanished, with the rest going over to the freethinkers.[33]

Many nineteenth-century religious movements, such as those of Christian revival, confessionalism, chiliasm, fundamentalism and Pentecostalism, successfully established denominations that exist to this day alongside the mainstream churches; and some religious groups that have their roots in the nineteenth century, like the Mormons, the New Apostolic Church and the Jehovah's Witnesses, are founded on principles that seem quite absurd. Why did these succeed while rationalism did not, though it was a rather broad movement?

I believe the reason for this is that religious rationalism is not a genuine religious idea, but the application of another idea to an existing religion. It is the notion of mediating between religion, plausibility in modern terms and usefulness – of a religion keeping abreast of intellectual and moral development.

---

**31** Hase 1834:11, 27–43; Hase 1837:1–2, 8, 15, 69–70, 75–84, 89–90.

**32** Cf. Elert 1921:159–212.

**33** Cf. Kampe 1852–1860; Pitzer 1983; Uhlig 1991.

Rationalism can show how a religion should be reformed to fit the claims of modern thinking, but it may itself persist in thinking in a way that is no longer modern. Even more importantly, it can hardly maintain something as unconditionally valid, or make it evident why you should follow a certain path or doctrine, or why you should join a certain group to escape damnation. Rational and perhaps also liberal Christianity can be an important element within a broader church, but it cannot maintain itself as a community in its own right.

## References


Aner, Karl. 1929. *Die Theologie der Lessingzeit*. Halle: Niemeyer.

Bachmann, Johannes. 1880. *Ernst Wilhelm Hengstenberg*, II. Gütersloh: Bertelsmann.

Barth, Karl. 1952. *Die protestantische Theologie im 19. Jahrhundert*[2]. Zollikon–Zurich: Evangelischer Verlag.

Beutel, Albrecht. 2009. *Kirchengeschichte im Zeitalter der Aufklärung*. Göttingen: Vandenhoeck & Ruprecht.

Elert, Werner. 1921. *Der Kampf um das Christentum*. Munich: Beck.

Hahn, August. 1827. *De rationalismi qui dicitur vera indole et qua cum naturalismo contineatur ratione*, I. Leipzig: Vogel.

Hase, Karl. 1833. *Hutterus redivivus oder Dogmatik der evangelisch-lutherischen Kirche*[2]. Leipzig: Leich.

Hase, Karl. 1834. *Theologische Streitschriften*. Leipzig: Breitkopf & Härtel.

Hase, Karl. 1837. *Anti-Röhr*[2] (Theologische Streitschriften, 3). Leipzig: Breitkopf & Härtel.

Hoffmann, Heinrich. 1908. "Wegscheider, Julius August Ludwig." In: *Realencyklopädie für protestantische Theologie und Kirche*[3]. Leipzig: Hinrichs. XXI:34–37, s.v.

Kampe, Ferdinand. 1852–1860. *Geschichte der religiösen Bewegung der neuern Zeit*, I–II. Leipzig: Wigand. III–IV. Leipzig: Wagner.

Kant, Immanuel. 1794. *Die Religion innerhalb der Grenzen der bloßen Vernunft*[2]. Königsberg: Nicolovius.

Kant, Immanuel. 1907. *Die Religion innerhalb der Grenzen der bloßen Vernunft: Die Metaphysik der Sitten*, ed. Georg Wobbermin and Paul Natorp (Akademie-Ausgabe, 6 = I/6). Berlin: Reimer.

Kant, Immanuel. 1996. *Religion and Rational Theology*, English transl. by Allan W. Wood and George di Giovanni (Cambridge Edition of the Works of Immanuel Kant, 6). Cambridge: Cambridge University Press.

Marheineke, Philipp. 1827 [1819]. *Die Grundlehren der christlichen Dogmatik*[2]. Berlin: Duncker & Humblot.

Pitzer, Volker. 1983. "Freireligiöse Bewegungen." In: *Theologische Realenzyklopädie*. Berlin West–New York: De Gruyter. XI:567–572, s.v.

Reinhard, Franz Volkmar. 1810. *Geständnisse seine Predigten und seine Bildung zum Prediger betreffend in Briefen an einen Freund*. Sulzbach: Seidel.

Röhr, Johann Friedrich. 1813. *Briefe über den Rationalismus*, Aix-la-Chapelle: Frosch.

Röhr, Johann Friedrich. 1836. *Anti-Hasiana oder Sammlung der Recensionen der Krit. Pred. Bibliothek, durch welche die Streitschriften des Hrn. Prof. D. Hase zu Jena veranlaßt wurden*. Neustadt an der Orla: Wagner.

Rohls, Jan. 1997. *Protestantische Theologie der Neuzeit*, I. Tübingen: Mohr (Siebeck).

Schelling, Friedrich Wilhelm Joseph. 1803. *Vorlesungen über die Methode des akademischen Studium*. Tübingen: Cotta.

Schelling, Friedrich Wilhelm Joseph. 1859. 1802, 1803 (Sämmtliche Werke, I/5). Stuttgart–Augustborough (Augsburg): Cotta.

[Schleiermacher, Friedrich.] 1799. *Über die Religion*. Berlin: Unger.

Schleiermacher, Friedrich. 1830–1831 [1821–1822]. *Der christliche Glaube nach den Grundsäzen der evangelischen Kirche im Zusammenhange dargestellt*[2]. I–II. Berlin: Reimer.

Schleiermacher, Friedrich. 1984. *Schriften aus der Berliner Zeit, 1796–1799*, ed. Günter Meckenstock (Kritische Gesamtausgabe, I/2). Berlin West–New York: De Gruyter.

Schleiermacher, Friedrich. 1996. *On Religion*[2], English transl. by Richard Crouter. Cambridge: University Press.

Uhlig, Christian. 1991. "Lichtfreunde." In: *Theologische Realenzyklopädie*. Berlin–New York: De Gruyter. XXI:119–121, s.v.

Wegscheider, Julius. 1804. *Ueber die von der neusten Philosophie geforderte Trennung der Moral von Religion*. Hamburg: Bohn.

Wegscheider, Julius. 1833. *Institutiones theologiae Christianae dogmaticae*[7]. Halle: Gebauer.

Johannes Zachhuber

# Individual and Community in Modern Debates about Religion and Secularism

## Introduction

Many scholars view the individualization or privatization of religion as one of the chief religious responses to modernity.[1] If, herein, I sound a somewhat dissenting note with regard to this well-established view, that is not because I think it is altogether wrong. The phenomena and trends scholars from different fields have observed and summarized under the heading of "individualization" do exist and are significant. In important ways, religion has become a matter of personal decision; it is seen as properly a concern of the individual. This growing conviction is perhaps most impressively seen in the rise of "religious freedom" as a fundamental – some would argue the most fundamental[2] – human right, but one could equally point to the increasing disconnect between membership in religious institutions and professed beliefs and practices to illustrate the same tendency.[3] It is certainly plausible to trace these elements of the contemporary religious landscape back to earlier Western developments, the very ones that are usually identified with the rise of modernity.[4]

Yet if this narrative has some claim to be true, I would nevertheless maintain that it represents only one part of the story. We do not fully understand the relationship between religion and modernity unless we perceive that alongside and together with a concern for religious individualism, there has also been a powerful dynamic at work that ties religion to the cohesion of communities.[5] We can see this tendency at work in our own age and time, where Orthodox Christianity has been marshalled in aid of collective identity in countries such as Russia or Ukraine,[6] to say nothing of the role political Islam has played in many places

1 Cf., classically, Parsons 1966. Individuation or privatization has also been cited in the context of theories of secularization; cf., e.g., Luckmann 1967; Luhmann 1977 and more recently Bruce 2002. For an overview of the debate and a critique of this line of argument cf. Casanova 1994:35–39.
2 This was the influential argument of Jellinek 1895. Cf. Joas 2011.
3 Cf., e.g., Pew Forum 2008.
4 Casanova 1994:37–38.
5 Zachhuber 2020.
6 Leustean 2014; Fagan 2012.

https://doi.org/10.1515/9783110723984-002

around the world. The same principle is applied, albeit in a less aggressive, more inclusive way, by the defenders of religious establishment, the unique association of a nation with one specific Church, in the United Kingdom and elsewhere.[7]

Furthermore, it seems evident that this latter line of thought has its own history, accompanying modernity as much as the narrative of individualization. It is a story in which concern about the loss of social cohesion is closely aligned with the observation of religious transformation: first the fracturing of the *Corpus Christianum* across Europe, then the toleration of a plurality of Christian churches within individual countries, followed by Jewish emancipation, the full embrace of religious pluralism, and finally secularism.

The obvious rejoinder to the construction of this "response" to modernity is that it describes not a modern response to religion, but the defensive reaction of those to whom modernity is unpalatable. The appeal to the communal dimension of religion as a remedy against society's tendency to disintegrate, it will be said, has been the characteristic strategy of the foes of the modern age, from the theorists of the French Restoration, such as de Maistre,[8] and romantics, such as Novalis,[9] to the Catholic opponents of modernism at the turn of the twentieth century, to the intellectual conservatives of our own time, such as Brad Gregory, who, in *The Unintended Reformation*, traces the fragmented nature of contemporary Western society (and practically all its other unpleasant features) back to the breakup of Europe's religious unity in the sixteenth century.[10]

This objection, however, overlooks two important facts. First, the notion that religion functions as a social bond tying together the members of a community is by no means restricted to conservative critics of modernity; it is shared by progressive thinkers such as Jean-Jacques Rousseau, Auguste Comte and Émile Durkheim, the last arguably the most influential theorist of religion along these lines since the early twentieth century. Second, a conception of modernity that excludes the "anti-modernists" is undialectical and simplistic, insofar as skepticism and hostility toward modernity are very much part of its history, regardless of when we let that history begin.[11] Contrary to some genealogical narratives, there never was a time when modernity was simply embraced, or when people were universally optimistic or enthusiastic about impending changes. Rather,

**7** Biggar 2014.

**8** Cf. Berlin 2003:131–154.

**9** Novalis 1968; Garrard 2004:55-63.

**10** Gregory 2015.

**11** The classic argument for this position it to be found in Horkheimer and Adorno 1997, but cf. Spaemann 1998.

any conception of modernity – and I readily admit that there is no agreed definition, to put it mildly – cannot do without the notion of fundamental change and transformation, and, consequently, the recognition that such developments always generated both optimism and pessimism, feelings of pride, achievement and, occasionally, hubris, but equally a lingering sense of loss, lack of orientation and even despair. Simply put, modernity was never just celebrated or just condemned, never simply affirmed or simply rejected. Its assessment was and remains ambivalent.

This ambivalence has by no means been restricted to the relationship between individual and society; one could easily describe attitudes toward technological progress or material wealth analogously. Yet there can be no doubt that this particular pair of polarities has provided one of the main arenas in which the conflict over the meaning and significance of modernity has played out. In this paper, I will therefore argue that a better understanding of religious responses to modernity is achieved if, instead of focussing exclusively on individualization, we examine the characterization of religion's role in the tension between the individual and society.

## Political Theology in Antiquity: Varro and Augustine

To substantiate my thesis about religion in modernity, I begin with the celebrated critique by Augustine of Hippo (354–430 CE) of the Roman author Marcus Terentius Varro's (116–27 BCE) exposition of political theology as one of three kinds of theology. The doctrine of the three genera of theology was, it seems, of Stoic origin, but most of our knowledge about it derives from Varro's treatise, which, in its turn, is principally known to us from Augustine's *City of God*.[12] Varro distinguished political theology from mythical theology, on the one hand, and physical or natural theology, on the other. However, we must not think that *theologia* in this context means what "theology" has come to denote in our own time – a discipline or field of enquiry. Rather, we need to take it literally, as signifying a discourse about God or the gods. The threefold division, then, seems initially not much more than the recognition that there are different contexts in which the gods are invoked, namely, the theater, philosophy and the state. This raises the question of how these contexts are related, and Varro's account, in a mix of the descriptive and the normative, sought to provide an answer to that question. Political theology, he suggested, partook in both the mythical and the philosophical. It had to, in

12 Augustine 1998:246–251; Rüpke 2005.

order to fulfil its role for the state: It appeals to public emotions by drawing on the gods of popular imagination, while preventing untoward consequences for the commonwealth by a moral adjudication of mythical religion, which is ultimately dependent on the natural theology of philosophers.[13]

The Christian apologist Augustine categorically rejected this line of reasoning. According to him, the pagan theory failed because, by its own admission, it depended on a system of myths that Varro himself acknowledged to be embarrassingly mendacious:

> The mythical theology, then – that of the theatrical performances, full of unworthiness and vileness – is referred back to the political: The whole of the mythical theology, rightly judged worthy of condemnation and rejection, is part of the political theology, which is deemed [sc. by Varro] worthy to be cultivated and observed.[14]

Augustine's alternative proposal is not without significance for my argument, and I shall briefly return to it at the end of this paper. For the moment, however, something else is more important: Neither he nor – from what we can gather – his pagan predecessor was primarily concerned with religion as a glue for societies, preventing them from disintegrating. While internal strife may well have been a possible source of political decline, it was certainly not in any way singled out as the one crucial danger to the polity, and political theology – whatever it may be – is therefore not primarily introduced as an ideology to guarantee social and political cohesion in the first instance.

Instead, the underlying concept is much broader, geared toward an understanding of the politician as someone informed by philosophers but capable of communicating with the population at large. Political theology is inscribed precisely into this mediating space and is deemed necessary because religion holds such strong affective power over people. It can therefore mislead the masses, but it is also capable of giving them moral direction. This tension calls for resolution, and on this the pagan and the Christian author disagree: Whereas Varro accepts the dichotomy between "immoral" popular religion and philosophical theology and therefore ascribes to the politician the art of bridging this divide, Augustine protests that without a unitary religion underlying all its various manifestations, no such harmony could ever obtain.

---

**13** Augustine 1998:248–249.

**14** Augustine 1998:251 (with changes).

## Political Theology in the Early Modern Period and the Fear of Political Disintegration

Varro's threefold scheme was an important point of reference for early modern discussions of natural and political theology, but the kind of concern these authors had for political theology was very different.[15] In the context of the religious wars and the emergence of modern nation states, the fear of political disintegration and the question of the public role of religion had emerged as closely related problems. To all early modern theorists, from Hobbes and Spinoza to Locke and Rousseau, the most fundamental conceptual difficulty to be solved was how human beings as individuals could form a stable political community. However much their responses differed, all these thinkers agreed on an anthropology for which the tension between human individuality and community cohesion was an unquestionable fact. It was this tension that led the "authoritarian" school, from Thomas Hobbes to Carl Schmitt, to endorse a powerful state with wide-ranging sovereignty over its citizens; but the same anthropology also inspired liberals who advocated individual freedom and individual human rights as protections of the citizen against the overweening authority of the government.

It goes beyond the purview of the present paper to argue in detail that these two traditions of political thought were two sides of the same coin, as has sometimes been claimed, but it is crucial for my purpose to observe that both linked the philosophical polarity of individual and community with the experience of social and political turmoil in the two centuries after the Reformation. This same combination, I believe, explains how religion was added to the mix. Once again, responses differed sharply. Some argued that religion had to be removed from the political realm, because it was religious disagreement that had previously led to violent conflict. As religious division apparently could not be overcome, it had to be prevented from undermining political peace and stability. This was the argument that eventually led to the idea of the privatization of religion.

This line of thought was expressed with aplomb in the so-called *Political Testament* of the Prussian king Frederick the Great. First published in 1752, the text describes Frederick's religious policies as follows:

> Lutherans, Catholics, Reformed, Jews and many other Christian sects live in Prussia, and they coexist peacefully. If the ruler had the idea, out of misplaced zeal, to favour one of them, at once there would be parties, and rows would erupt ...

---

15 Stroumsa 2010:152. On modern political theology cf. also: Schmitt 1970 and 1979; Kantorowicz 1957; Arendt 1958; Vega 2017.

> For politics it is altogether unimportant whether the ruler is religious or not. If one gets to the bottom of any religion, they are all founded on a more or less irrational system of fables. ... However, one must be careful not to hurt the religious feelings of the big masses whatever their religion.
> I am, so to speak, the pope of the Lutherans and the ecclesiastical head of the reformed. All the other Christian sects are tolerated in Prussia. The first one trying to unleash a civil war must at once be silenced, and the teachings of the would-be reformer will be exposed to ridicule.[16]

Here, a plurality of religions is acknowledged and accepted as a social reality. Potentially negative consequences for political stability are staved off by ruthless state control imposed on religious groups. At the same time, the state is technically "secular," as Frederick makes clear through his rather astonishing claim that the personal religion of the monarch is irrelevant.

Yet it was not difficult to argue, based on the same concern for political stability, that a unified religion was needed after all, as without it an integrated polity was impossible to attain. Frederick, of course, represents Enlightenment principles. Throughout the seventeenth and for much of the eighteenth century, however, most of the early modern nation states followed the alternative approach, so much so that one may well ask to what extent their policy of religious homogenization was a response to the horrors of the religious wars, or whether the latter rather provided a convenient pretext for a policy aimed at the consolidation of national power.[17] But that is not my topic here.

My concern instead is the conceptualization of religion that emerged in this situation. As in the case of political theory, it is arguable that radically divergent responses shared an underlying theoretical consensus. In the case of religion, this consensus emphasized the significance of the polarity of individual and community. Confusingly, religion appeared as both individual and communal; it could therefore both stabilize and destabilize a society. The political theologian had to explain this state of affairs and offer a solution to the conundrum it created. It is this constellation, I would argue, that gave rise to the specifically modern link posited between religion and community cohesion. In what follows, I shall show how major thinkers since the eighteenth century developed this idea in rather different ways.

---

16 Frederick the Great 1974:44–45. My translation from the German – J.Z.

17 Cavanaugh 2009.

## Jean-Jacques Rousseau: Apolitical Christianity and the Need for a Political Religion

Jean-Jacques Rousseau discusses the significance of religion for the state in a rightly famous chapter of *The Social Contract*.[18] He sought to resolve the paradox of religion as a source of both stability and instability by distinguishing between different types of religion. According to him, it was the emergence of Judeo-Christian monotheism that fatally undermined the political function of religion. As long as every city and country had its own god, there were no religious wars – even though, technically, every war was also "theological" (p. 143) – because in the polytheistic system there was no distinction between the nation and its religion. Therefore, Rousseau argued, men did not so much fight for the gods; rather, the gods fought for men (p. 144). This was reversed with the emergence of a novel type of religion that was primarily based not on national identity but on universal truth:

> It was in these circumstances that Jesus came to establish a Spiritual Kingdom on earth; which, by separating the theological from the political system, led to the State's ceasing to be one, and caused the intestine divisions which have never ceased to convulse Christian peoples. (*ibid.*)

Christianity is therefore wholly unsuited as a national religion. Yet, and this is crucial, Rousseau continued to affirm the political need for universal religiosity: "It matters very much to the community that each citizen should have a religion; that will make him love his duty" (p. 150). For this reason, he advocated the introduction of a civil religion that would, among other things, demand religious toleration, so that in such a state all religions can peacefully coexist – provided, of course, that they foreswear political ambitions.

Crucial for my purpose here, however, is the precise function ascribed by Rousseau to political religion as he conceives it. Given the overall structure of his political thought, with its insistence on the necessity and centrality of the *volonté générale*, the general will,[19] the primacy he assigns to social cohesion should not surprise us. He repeatedly emphasizes the "bond of union" (p. 148) that religion is supposed to provide: the "great bond of particular societies" (p. 147). Yet he also judges religion anti-social, because "everything which destroys social unity is worthless" (*ibid.*) – a judgment that applies in particular to Roman Catholicism, a type of religion that "is so manifestly bad that it is a waste of time

**18** Rousseau 1997:142–151. Cf. Karant 2016; Beiner 2012:11–16 (and *passim*).
**19** Rousseau 1997:xx–xxii; 57–60.

to amuse oneself demonstrating that it is" (*ibid.*). It is both transnational and a state-like institution, and it therefore inevitably generates a rival claim to the citizens' loyalty.

At first sight, it could appear that Rousseau was merely pleading for a restoration of the pre-Christian, pagan acceptance of political religion as more or less separate from the people's religion, which must be tolerated in its plurality. Yet this would miss something rather important: Rousseau's distinction between civil and natural religion is almost entirely driven by his dichotomy of individual and society. He accepts the need for religion to underwrite social unity and cohesion while maintaining that ideal Christianity, which he believes is identical with natural religion, is entirely unsuited for this purpose. For this reason, the latter becomes a private affair, while the need for communal identity makes necessary a novel entity, civil religion.

## Catholicism and Political Stability in Restoration Thought

Moving from Rousseau into the nineteenth century, we find Catholic opponents of the French Revolution presenting a vision of society that, at first sight, is the exact opposite of Rousseau's program. The so-called Catholic Restoration, represented by individuals such as Joseph de Maistre,[20] Louis de Bonald[21] and Félicité de Lamennais,[22] aimed to reconstitute society on the basis of religion, more specifically Catholic Christianity. The reason for this is perhaps simple enough: Society's rebellion against the traditional order had led to chaos and terrible suffering; its underlying maxim therefore had to be reversed. On closer inspection, however, these thinkers are not nearly as categorically opposed to Rousseau as might first appear. An investigation of de Maistre and de Bonald will show that they share with their forerunner the assumption that religion is connected to communal cohesion. In fact, they radicalized this view.

### Joseph de Maistre

In his *Considérations sur la France*,[23] written in 1797, Joseph de Maistre railed against the "Decree on Religious Liberty" adopted by the Convention on February

---

**20** On de Maistre cf. Berlin 2003:131–154. Berlin's one-sided account has been challenged by Armenteros 2011 and Hedley 2011.

**21** On de Bonald cf. Spaemann 1998.

**22** On Lamennais cf. Derré 1962; Oldfield 1973; Armenteros 2011:232 ff.

**23** De Maistre 1831.

21, 1795, which stipulated the separation of church and state (p. 68). Such an idea, he argued, had never in the history of the world been promulgated, and with good reason: "All imaginable institutions rest on a religious idea, or they must pass away" (*ibid.*). Institutions are stable only to the extent that they are "divinized" (*divinisées*). Human intellectual endeavour and secular philosophy are not merely unable to substitute for those divine foundations; they are essentially a force of division and instability.

What "institutions" does the author have in mind? De Maistre takes a broad view, including the whole "chain of human establishments" from the grandest to the smallest, from empires to brotherhoods (*ibid.*, p. 70). In all these instances, he observes, "religion mixes itself with everything, it animates and sustains everything" (*ibid.*). While historically these institutions were founded by human individuals, their founders could not but somehow ally themselves with God in order to make their institutions stable and permanent. Try as they may, he argues, secular rulers could not even command their people to assemble regularly each year in a particular place to perform a dance. They would fail in such an endeavour, de Maistre writes, while the humble Christian missionary of the first millennium succeeded in inspiring religious festivals that continue two thousand years later.

This is de Maistre's challenge to the French Revolution, which in its "anti-religious character" is, as he put it, truly "satanic" (p. 67). By attacking the religious foundation of society, the revolutionaries took away what makes society into society. They removed the bond that holds people together, thus threatening not one particular form of government or one particular type of social organization, but society as such. The reason, de Maistre intimates, is that human beings are transient and therefore incapable of creating something that lasts. Their power is limited; even the mightiest monarch or the most extraordinary genius cannot institute a form of sociality without invoking divine help.

These insights, Maistre insists, are not specifically related to his own or anyone's religious faith:

> These reflections are addressed to everyone, believer and sceptic alike. I state a fact; I do not advance a hypothesis. Whether one laughs at these ideas or whether one worships them; rightly or wrongly they form the unique basis of all durable institutions. (p. 69)[24]

---

24 "Ces réflexions s'adressent à tout le monde, au croyant comme au sceptique; c'est un fait que j'avance et non une thèse." My translation – J.Z.

This is crucial. Whatever de Maistre's religious convictions, his argument does not appeal to them, nor is it explicitly meant to be theological. "The whole of history," he insists, teaches that institutions need a religious basis to succeed and become stable (pp. 69–70). Studying our European institutions "in depth" (*approfondir*) demonstrates that they are all "Christianized" (*christianisées*).

In keeping with the early modern tradition, then, de Maistre thinks of religion as fundamental to social cohesion and stability. In his response to the French Revolution, he especially emphasizes the connection between religion and social institutions. Two observations, however, set him apart from earlier reflections. First, his outlook is entirely historical. Institutions are considered in terms of their foundation, their growth and their endurance; religion is consistently inscribed into this historicist framework. Second, the religious character of institutions is aligned with the personal authority of the founder. It is always a person who allies himself with the divinity and is thus empowered to create a stable and durable institution (pp. 71–72).

These two specific aspects of de Maistre's view help explain his theoretical steps beyond the argument in the *Considérations*. Notwithstanding his generic references to a diversity of religions in his attack on the "satanic" Revolution, de Maistre by no means thought that all religions were created equal when it came to their social function. Ultimately, there was one religion perfectly suited to this role: Roman Catholicism. This tenet was the basis of de Maistre's case for Ultramontanism in his 1819 book *Du pape*.[25] Here, the author asserts that "the Christian religion is the only institution which knows no decay, because it alone is divine" (p. 22 [I 5]).[26] It is easy to see how this is simply an extension of the more universal principle for which he argued in his earlier work. Institutions can only have stability if their foundation is connected with God. Christianity alone is "divine," so it is the one institution that has eternal endurance.

There is, moreover, an important precondition for this institutional success: the papacy:

> Without the Pope, there is no true Christianity; – without the Pope, the Divine institution loses its power, its Divine character, and its converting influence; – without the Pope, it is nothing better than a system, a human belief, incapable of penetrating and modifying the

---

**25** De Maistre 1850.

**26** There is a tension between de Maistre's argument here that the Church is "always the same," unlike human institutions that have "their infancy, their manhood, their old age, and their end," and his subsequent insistence (in defence of the unseemly beginnings of the papacy) that "everything that exists legitimately and for ages, exists at first in germ, and is developed successively," *ibid.*:24 (I 6).

> heart, to render man susceptible of a higher degree of science, of morality and civilization. (p. 295 [III 8])

We saw before how, for de Maistre, the religious quality of any institution was explained in terms of a founder who aligned himself ("se mettant en rapport" – *Considérations*, p. 69) with God. This emphasis on the necessarily personal dimension of institutional cohesion – as opposed to Rousseau's impersonal *volontée générale* – is carried over from the political to the religious sphere without much ado:

> When every species of criticism has been exhausted, and when have been thrown, as is reasonable, into the other scale of the balance, all the advantages of monarchy, what is the final result? *It is the best, the most durable of governments, and the most natural to men.* Let the court of Rome be judged in the same way. It is a monarchy, the only possible form of government for ruling the Catholic Church. (*The Pope*, p. 298 [III 8])

Of course, not even de Maistre would argue that St. Peter was the founder of Christianity, but the parallel is evident nonetheless. Religion can ultimately provide its social benefits only if it is truly divine and represented by an institution ideally suited to the preservation of its social impulse.

De Maistre's theory was developed in conscious opposition to Rousseau, "l'homme du monde peut-être qui s'est le plus trompé" (*Considérations*, p. 69). And yet, if it was simplistic to see Rousseau as returning to a pre-Christian model of political theology, it would be equally facile to find in the opponent of the Revolution a mere antagonist of the political thought of his forebear. While it is true that de Maistre adopted the very model of religious affiliation that had seemed to Rousseau the most pernicious – Roman Catholicism – their most fundamental intuitions are remarkably similar. Both consider societies from the point of view of their risk of disintegration and their corresponding need for stability. Both likewise ascribe to religion a major part in this dialectic. Religion can and should contribute to social and political stability, but it can also have the opposite effect. Finally, neither of them conceals that their assessment of individual religions, or indeed of specific versions of Christianity, is primarily conditioned by the potential of those faiths to hinder or promote political and social integration.

### L.G.A. de Bonald

L.G.A. de Bonald is usually seen as following in the footsteps of de Maistre's line of thought; de Maistre himself acknowledged as much.[27] Yet the details of his sys-

---

27 Spaemann 1998:83. My reconstruction of de Bonald's role in this story is strongly indebted to Spaemann's masterful study.

tem are not always identical with the approach of his celebrated forerunner, and the mode in which he presents his ideas is rather different. Where de Maistre, the brilliant stylist, relished the paradoxical *bon mot*, de Bonald preferred the precise and dry language of the scholar. Like de Maistre, de Bonald identified the Revolution with both social anarchy and atheism. The collapse of political order, in his view, was directly related to the undermining of public religion.[28] It is therefore unsurprising that for him, too, religion is closely connected with the purpose of social and communal cohesion.

De Bonald hardly conceals his dependence on Rousseau, despite his equally fundamental criticism of the philosopher from Geneva.[29] Following Rousseau, de Bonald identifies the principle of social and political cohesion as the general will, a volition that is constantly in tension with the desires of individuals.[30] Yet the anti-revolutionary thinker argues that this *volonté générale* cannot be explained "from below," as the product of the infinite plurality of private wills (I, p. 130);[31] it has to be reconstructed as a transcendent reality that is always already present in any human community. Ultimately, then, for de Bonald, the general will is the will of God:

> Therefore, the general will of society, of the social body, of man as a social being; the nature of social being or of society; social will; even the will of God are all synonymous expressions. (I, p. 147)[32]

While de Bonald emphatically does not think that God is a human invention, it is nevertheless clear to him that, apart from His presence in society, God has no reality.[33] Consequently, de Bonald can speak of the "production" and "conservation" of God through society (I, p. 475) and assert that God is really and truly absent from an atheist nation (III, pp. 478–479).

If religion and society are thus perhaps more closely aligned in de Boland than in any previous thinker, this is the direct result of his concern with social and political stability. De Bonald agrees with Hobbes regarding the fragility of the political order (II, p. 13).[34] He pointedly affirms Hobbes's celebrated notion of

**28** In particular through modern philosophy. Cf. de Bonald 1859:3, 29.
**29** Spaemann 1998:73.
**30** *Ibid.*
**31** Cf. *ibid.*:74
**32** "Ainsi, volonté générale de la société, du corps social, de l'homme social, nature des êtres sociaux ou de la société, volonté sociale, volonté de Dieu même, sont des expressions synonymes …." My translation – J.Z..
**33** Spaemann 1998:119–120.
**34** *Ibid.*:104–105.

*bellum omnium contra omnes*, even if he denies that this was humanity's state of nature (II, p. 33, n. 3).[35] What was natural, he argues, was the opposite state, in which the selfish and destructive energies of human individuality were overcome by the imposition of an order fulfilling humanity's deepest need: self-preservation (III, p. 451).[36] This could only be achieved, however, by a spiritual power aligning human volition with the general will of the state. Thus far, religion and the political system were two sides of the same coin: it was therefore necessary, writes de Bonald, to consider political society from the point of view of religion, and religious society from the point of view of the political government (I, p. 327).[37]

This alignment of political and religious order was not, however, "natural," in the sense of being a universal fact of human history; it required the right institutions in its support. On the political side, it worked best with monarchy,[38] while on the religious side it was ultimately only Christianity, more specifically Roman Catholic Christianity, that perfectly fulfilled this function. De Bonald developed an elaborate political theology to support this contention. It was centered on the Incarnation as the guarantee of God's presence in the world and the Catholic Eucharist as the regular reenactment of Christ's sacrificial act of divine–human reconciliation.[39]

Like de Maistre, de Bonald attempted a philosophical justification of the restoration of the Bourbon monarchy. The French Revolution was not merely a political aberration, and a failed one at that; it was also living proof of the falseness of modern philosophy, with its "atheistic" tendencies (III, p. 40).[40] Only a return to the monarchy of the *ancien régime*, with its particularly close connection to French Catholicism, therefore, could heal the damage done to French society by the Revolution. Despite this conservative intention, however, de Bonald's position was much more ambiguous. As Robert Spaemann masterfully showed more than sixty years ago,[41] de Bonald's political theology paradoxically gave birth to sociology and thus to a much more radically secular approach to society and religion than had been broached by any eighteenth-century thinker. In many ways,

35 *Ibid.*:106.

36 "La société la plus civilisée est donc la société la plus naturelle, comme l'homme le plus perfectionné est l'homme le plus naturel." Cf. Spaeman 1998:67–68.

37 "Il faut [...] considérer la société politique sous le point de vue de la religion, et la société religieuse sous le point de vue du gouvernement politique."

38 Spaemann 1998:79–80.

39 *Ibid.*:121–122.

40 *Ibid.*:21–22.

41 *Ibid.* The title of Spaemann's study sums up his interpretation: the birth of sociology from the spirit of the Restoration.

de Bonald is a vital, albeit ironic, link between Hobbes and Rousseau, on the one hand, and Comte and Durkheim, on the other.[42]

To a large extent, this was a consequence of de Bonald's intuitive identification of religion as instrumental for social cohesion. As we have seen, he inherited this notion from a particular early modern constellation, which he both accepted and radicalized. Why, he wondered, could a disaster such as the French Revolution ever have happened? Despite his admiration for the *ancien régime* and his contempt for the Revolution, he believed that there was an insight that could be gained from his post-Revolution vantage point. Observing in real time how the application of the "atheistic" philosophy of the Enlightenment was able radically to undermine the old social and political order allowed one to perceive *for the first time* the intimate nature of the connection between religion and society (III, p. 447).[43]

Rousseau had seen in Christianity a radically other-worldly religion unsuitable for the political integration of the state. De Bonald went to the opposite extreme, so to speak, by closely aligning Christianity with the principle of social and political unity and integration. In the process, he turned religion into a function of society, albeit its most fundamental function. The reality of God is collapsed into the totality of society, whose unitive and rational principle He becomes. While de Bonald believed this to be a vindication of Roman Catholicism in its traditional alliance with the Bourbon throne, it does not take much to see that the same tenets could easily be conscripted into the service of a rather different philosophy as well.

## Religion and Social Cohesion: The Secular Version

The direction in which my narrative is tending is perhaps by now becoming clear. If religion is taken to be so closely aligned with the cohesion of a community, a nation or a society, then its failure to deliver this result becomes its failure *qua* religion. One might argue that the thinkers of the Catholic Restoration were in a way setting themselves up for failure, insofar as the society in which they existed was

42 For this argument cf. also Milbank 2006:55–60.

43 De Bonald uses the powerful metaphor of a storm to illustrate "cette commotion universelle, [...] ce renversement du monde sociale, qui, mettant a découvert le fond même de la société." It is "semblable à ces tempêtes violentes qui soulèvent l'Océan jusque dans les plus profonds abîmes, et laissent voir les bancs énormes de roche qui en supportent et en contiennent les eaux." Cf. Spaemann 1998:39–40.

simply unwilling to embrace Catholicism as unanimously as their theory seemed to require. It is therefore not difficult to see how their ultra-conservative theory could, by a further ironic twist, give rise to a theory of secularization. All that was needed at that point was the assumption, empirical in a way, that Catholic Christianity had in fact lost its sway over the population at large.

This modification seems first to have been proposed by Henri de Saint-Simon. In his *Introduction aux travaux scientifiques du dix-neuvième siècle*,[44] he declared himself full of admiration for de Bonald's writings, "the most estimable productions that have been brought to light in many years" (I, p. 211). He explicitly endorsed de Bonald's emphasis on what he calls the "utility of a unitive system" that can hold society together. Yet he was unconvinced that this unity could be provided by the traditional idea of God (*déisme*). In a rapid historical overview, Saint-Simon described modern Western history as a story in which Christianity increasingly found itself intellectually on the back foot, unable in particular to compete with the newly emerging paradigm of science (pp. 208–211). It was science, therefore, in particular Newton's law of gravity, that conceivably could provide the strong unitive bond that Christianity used to offer (p. 212).

This line of thought was subsequently taken up by Auguste Comte in his *Système de politique positive ou traité de sociologie*.[45] Comte's intellectual debt both to Saint-Simon and to the Restoration thinkers, which seems beyond doubt, has been variously interpreted. While Robert Spaemann, Robert Nisbet, John Milbank and, most recently, Carolina Armenteros have proposed a strong albeit paradoxical link between anti-revolutionary thought and later French social science, Pierre Macherey and Anthony Giddens have sought to downplay the connection.[46]

For my present purpose it is not necessary to take sides in this controversy. According to Comte, religion is "the state of full harmony appropriate to human existence" (p. 8). This harmony extends to the two main dualities characteristic of human life: mind and body, and individual and society. It would therefore be too simple to reduce Comte's view to the notion that religion holds society together, but the latter idea undoubtedly plays an important part in his theory. Religion reins in and rallies together (*régler*, *rallier*) individuals, as Comte constantly emphasizes (*ibid.*). In other words, it suppresses selfish impulses while instilling

44 Saint-Simon 1859.

45 Comte 1852.

46 Spaemann 1998:184–185; Nisbet 2004:xii, 57; Milbank 2006:55; Armenteros 2017; Macherey 1991:41–47; Giddens 1972. Giddens' main concern, however, is with Durkheim. He expressly concedes that "Comte drew upon the ideas of the 'conservative' Catholic apologists" and especially so in the *Positive Polity* (*ibid.*:363); "but it was Comte's *Positive Philosophy* which particularly influenced Durkheim" (*ibid.*).

into individuals a real desire to serve the whole. For this reason, it has to work on both the heart and the mind, by including doctrine as well as cult.

Historical religions, Comte argued, had a mixed record with regard to these functions. He eschewed the neat evolutionism found in the thinking of some of his contemporaries and notably believed that monotheism had a dangerous tendency towards the doctrinal, making it overly intellectual and ultimately egotistical and sectarian.[47] This adverse potential of monotheistic religion became most pronounced, he thought, in Protestantism, probably the faith he detested more than any other.[48] Catholicism, by contrast, came closest to perfection, partly because it retained salutary elements of polytheism and fetishism, such as the cult of saints and, notably, the veneration of the Virgin Mary (p. 134).[49] Catholicism was also most advanced in its hierarchical structure, which was necessary because religion was geared towards social unity.

Ultimately, none of the historical religions succeeded in realizing its full potential, however. This only became possible on the basis of scientific insight elucidating the deep connections between humanity's physical, biological and psychological constitutions. The key to this unity, Comte believed, lay in a new field, for which he famously coined the term "social science" (pp. 52–53). Elucidating the laws governing this reality, which he himself had discovered, would finally be able to replace traditional theology as the queen of sciences, engineering a society in a state of perfect harmony. For this project, Comte coined the phrase "religion of humanity."[50]

Despite the idiosyncrasies of his thought, it is easy to see how Comte fits into the narrative of my paper and also extends it. Like de Maistre and de Bonald, he wrote in the shadow of the French Revolution, deeply worried about the breakdown of social and political order.[51] Added to this trauma is his awareness of the social disruptions of early capitalism.[52] Like Rousseau, he saw Christianity as ambiguous in its political and social consequences, but he followed the Restoration theorists *against* the early modern consensus, espoused by Rousseau, in his assessment of the relative merits of Catholicism. Like Saint-Simon, finally, he combined an appreciation of the socially stabilizing character of the Catholic sys-

---

**47** Lubac 1995:183–186; Wernick 2004:110–111, with nn. 61–62.

**48** Lubac 1995:204–205.

**49** "Le catholicisme, qu'on pourrait justement nommer le polythéisme du moyen âge ...." Cf. Lubac 1995:197–198.

**50** Cf. Wernick 2004. The full title of Comte's 1852 work is *Système du politique positive, ou Traité de sociologie, Instituant la religion de l'humanité.*

**51** Nisbet 2004:57.

**52** Wernick 2004:81.

tem with the idea that scientific progress had made even this form of traditional religion untenable.

Of all Comte's ideas, none has earned him more ridicule than his attempt to set up a new religious cult with himself as its head. Despite the abject failure of the cult of humanity as a putative replacement for traditional religion and a scientifically based church for the modern world, however, Comte's project was not without some remarkable effects. Comte himself dreamt of a "holy alliance" between positivists and Catholics,[53] and the same consideration inspired the personally agnostic Charles Maurras in his foundation of the notorious Action Française.[54] In the thick of the Dreyfus affair, Maurras sought to rally together all those willing to recreate a traditional, monarchical France as a "Christian society." By Christian he meant, similarly to Comte, the medieval, Catholic transformation of a religion that in its origins was deeply tainted by anarchic tendencies, which Maurras identified with Judaism. Due to its Jewish origin, the biblical text itself "will always operate in a Jewish manner unless it is interpreted by Rome."[55]

The spirit of the Action Française was, unsurprisingly, alien to Émile Durkheim, son of a rabbi, defender of Colonel Dreyfus and lifelong republican.[56] Yet the notion of religion as the bond that holds society together stands nevertheless at the center of his celebrated sociological theory as well. In fact, the significance of this notion for Durkheim's thought is so evident and so well known that further elaboration on this point seems unnecessary in the present context.[57] It has often been observed that Durkheim's interest in religion dates only from a late period in his career. Much earlier, however, in his works on the division of labor and on suicide, he had mused about what he called *l'anomie*, normlessness, as a radical threat to social cohesion.[58]

Thus far, his later account of religion, as offered in *The Elementary Forms of Religious Life* (1912),[59] inscribes itself into the trajectory of modern thought, which accorded to religion a crucial role in community cohesion in response to the fear that society would disintegrate. Throughout the extensive analyses by means of which Durkheim sought to establish his view of religion, this broader agenda retreats into the background. Yet it is spelt out with admirable clarity in the rightly

**53** Lubac 1995:204–214.
**54** Spaemann 1998:186–188.
**55** Maurras 1978:24.
**56** Giddens 1972:361.
**57** Cf., e.g., Hausner 2017.
**58** Durkheim 1930a:360–365; 1930b:264–311.
**59** Durkheim 1995.

famous words in the book's final chapter in which Durkheim gives expression to his assessment of the religious situation of his own time:

> The great things of the past which filled our fathers with enthusiasm do not excite the same zeal in us, either because they have passed so completely into common custom that we lose awareness of them or because they no longer suit our aspirations. Meanwhile no replacement to them has as yet been created. [...] In short, the former gods are growing old or dying, and others have not been born. This is what voided Comte's attempt to organize a religion using old historical memories, artificially revived. It is life itself, and not a dead past, that can produce a living cult. But that state of uncertitude and confused anxiety cannot last forever. A day will come when our societies once again will know hours of creative effervescence, during which new ideas will again spring forth and new formulas emerge to guide humanity for a time. (p. 429)

Here, the view of religion as community cohesion has, *faute de mieux*, mutated into a theory of secularization. Note the reference to Comte, surely not coincidentally inserted into this key passage. It is hard not to read it dialectically as expressing a sense of solidarity with the earlier theorist, alongside the overt criticism. Comte, Durkheim seems to say, was right to identify the retreat of religion as a severe problem; he was right, moreover, to diagnose the state of traditional Christianity as one of advanced decay. Yet he erred in his belief that it was the task of the theorist to remedy this situation, because ultimately "it is [only] life itself [...] that can produce a living cult." The modern predicament is thus understood as indicating a profoundly theological "absence of God," for whose return humanity can only wait. Secularization, then, will not last forever, but it is the current reality, to which the reader of the book is prompted to acquiesce.

While this religious diagnosis appears only as an afterthought to Durkheim's actual, scientific analysis in the *Elementary Forms*, the core of his theory of religion is – just as it was in Rousseau and in the thinkers of the Catholic Restoration – the idea that religion is what binds society together. As a matter of fact, Durkheim adopts the more radical view, adumbrated by de Bonald and Comte, according to which religion *is* society in its integrated state. To that extent, Durkheim's diagnosis of the religious situation in France's Third Republic is yet another response to the deeply engrained fear of social destabilization, which, throughout the modern period, was the backdrop to theories emphasizing the socially and politically stabilizing role of religion.

## Conclusion: Augustine and the Problem of Religious Diversity

Throughout this paper, I have attempted to follow the trajectory of the early modern alignment of religious unity and social and political stability. By starting from

Varro's notion of political theology, I showed how pre-Christian antiquity saw the problematic relationship between religion and politics in a characteristically different light. The political theologian had to mediate between the powerfully affective but superstitious religion of the masses and the philosophical religion of the elite. This theory responded to tensions between types of religion, each suitable for a different social sphere. While it would be wrong to say that the perception reflected in Varro's theory was entirely absent from later Western political thought, it is fundamentally incompatible with the principles of Christianity. As Augustine clearly articulated, the Christian faith, in this regard following the example of biblical Judaism, could not tolerate a duality of elite and popular religion.

When this unified theological vision came under strain in early modernity, the fault line was no longer the duality of folk religion and philosophical religion. Instead, in line with the predominant theoretical concern about the integration and disintegration of societies, it was asked what role religion had to play in this connection. Consequently, religion was inscribed into the tension between individuality and community, and the question to be answered was whether it contributed to social stability or led to fragmentation. This then led to a strand of theorists seeking to understand religion specifically in its cohesive function for societies.

As I have shown, this line of thought served very different purposes – from Rousseau's liberal Enlightenment perspective to the conservatism of the Catholic Restoration to Durkheim's theory of secularization. None of them, it seems to me, well captures the particular way in which religion is a matter of the individual in community with others. Instead, religion is forced into a procrustean bed fashioned by the foundational concern of modern political and social theory with social stability and cohesion. As religion had been crucial to the political and social upheavals of early modernity, this perspective is perhaps not surprising, but from our historical distance, its limitations are nonetheless striking.

Understanding religions in this way subordinated them to the strategies of politicians and nationalist activists. It made the messages of religions indistinguishable from the founding myths of states and nations. Religious minorities – Jews, French Protestants, German Catholics – fared even worse, as their faiths in this perspective looked not merely theologically erroneous but like perversions of religion. Religious minorities were not only wrong but dangerous; their very existence inevitably called into question the stability and durability of the social and political commonwealth. Ultimately, the association of religion with communal cohesion was also pragmatically self-defeating. The empirical increase in religious diversity and the nostalgic longing for religious homogeneity became intertwined elements of a narrative that with some logic led to the view that, due to the absence of a unified church, modernity spelt the end of religion. Durkheim's affirmation of secularization *in this regard* seems entirely plausible.

Is this problematic, then, exclusively a result of the idiosyncrasies of Western modernity? I think such a conclusion might ultimately be too simplistic. Let us recall why Augustine thought he could reject Varro's plurality of theologies. By providing a single narrative and a single theory encompassing equivalents of all three "theologies," Christianity promised a more durable and reliable foundation for the existence of the commonwealth than Varro's Roman ideology ever could. From the outset, then, Christian political theology was much more ambitious than that of Roman paganism, in combining popular imagination, political functionality and philosophical reflection into one. Where Varro's politician mediated between ultimately incommunicable visions of popular and philosophical religion, Augustine's project entailed the need for the philosopher-theologian to educate not only the prince, but also the population at large.

This argument undoubtedly is powerful, yet there is no denying that its success largely depended on the sociologically unifying power of the Christian Church – and in practice that meant the Church's close collaboration with the state. While Varro's system accepted the irreducible diversity and plurality of popular religion as a built-in assumption, in Augustine's alternative proposal, religious division became a political problem.

This does not make all these modern theorists Augustinians, but, in viewing a single, shared religion as the key for political unity, they all grappled with a problem bequeathed to Western political thought by the bishop of Hippo. It was the demise of his unified vision over the course of modernity that seemed to call for compensation. Perhaps ironically, the end result of these compensatory theories turned out to be rather detrimental to religion.

## References

Arendt, Hannah. 1958. *The Human Condition*. Chicago: University of Chicago Press.

Armenteros, Carolina. 2011. *The French Idea of History: Joseph de Maistre and His Heirs (1794–1854)*. Ithaca: Cornell University Press.

Armenteros, Carolina. 2017. "The Counterrevolutionary Comte: Theorist of Two Powers and Enthusiastic Medievalist." In: Andrew Wernick (ed.), *The Anthem Companion to Auguste Comte*. London: Anthem Press. 91–116.

Augustine of Hippo. 1998. *The City of God against the Pagans* (English transl. by R.W. Dyson). Cambridge: Cambridge University Press.

Beiner, Ronald. 2012. *Civil Religion: A Dialogue in the History of Political Philosophy*. Cambridge: Cambridge University Press.

Berlin, Isaiah. 2003. *Freedom and Its Betrayal: Six Enemies of Human Liberty*, ed. Henry Hardy. Missoula: Pimlico.

Biggar, Nigel. 2014. *Between Kin and Cosmopolis: An Ethic of the Nation*. Eugene, OR: Cascade.
de Bonald, L.G.A. 1859. *Oeuvres Complètes*, ed. J.-P. Migne. I–III. Montrouge: J.-P. Migne.
Bruce, Steve. 2002. *God Is Dead: Secularization in the West*. Oxford: Blackwell
Casanova, Jose. 1994. *Public Religions in the Modern World*. Chicago: University of Chicago Press.
Cavanaugh, William. 2009. *The Myth of Religious Violence: Secular Ideology and the Roots of Modern Conflict*. Oxford: Oxford University Press.
Comte, Auguste. 1852. *Système de politique positive ou traité de sociologie*. II. Paris: Carillian-Goeury/Dalmont.
Derré, Jean-René. 1962. *Lamennais, ses amis et le movement des idées à l'époque romantique (1824–1834)*. Paris: Klincksieck.
Durkheim, Émile. 1930a. *De la division du travail social*. Paris: Presses Universitaires de France.
Durkheim, Émile. 1930b. *Le suicide*. Paris: Presses Universitaires de France.
Durkheim, Émile. 1995. *The Elementary Forms of Religious Life* (English transl. by Karen E. Fields). New York: Free Press.
Fagan, Geraldine. 2012. *Believing in Russia: Religious Policy after Communism*. London: Routledge.
Frederick the Great. 1974 [1752]. *Testament politique*. German edition: *Das Politische Testament von 1752*. Stuttgart: Reclam.
Garrard, Graeme. 2004. *Counter-Enlightenments: From the Eighteenth Century to the Present*. London: Routledge.
Giddens, Anthony. 1972. "Four Myths in the History of Social Thought." *Economy and Society*, 1:357–385.
Gregory, Brad S. 2015. *The Unintended Reformation: How a Religious Revolution Secularized Society*. Cambridge, MA: Harvard University Press.
Hausner, Sondra L. 2017. "Is Individual to Collective as Freud is to Durkheim?" In *eadem* (ed.), *Durkheim in Dialogue: A Centenary Celebration of* The Elementary Forms of Religious Life. New York–London: Berghahn, 167–179.
Hedley, Douglas. 2011. *Sacrifice Imagined: Violence, Atonement, and the Sacred*. London: Bloomsbury.
Horkheimer, Max, and Theodor W. Adorno. 1997. *Dialectic of Enlightenment* (English transl. by John Cumming). New York: Continuum.
Jellinek, Georg. 1895. *Die Erklärung der Menschen- und Bürgerrechte: Ein Beitrag zur modernen Verfassungsgeschichte*. Leipzig: Duncker & Humblot.
Joas, Hans. 2011. *Die Sakralität der Person: Eine neue Genealogie der Menschenrechte*. Frankfurt/M.: Suhrkamp.
Kantorowicz, Ernst. 1957. *The King's Two Bodies: A Study in Medieval Political Theology*. Princeton: Princeton University Press.
Karant, Joshua. 2016. "Revisiting Rousseau's Civil Religion." *Philosophy and Social Criticism*, 42:1028–1058.
Leustean, Lucian N. 2014. *Eastern Christianity and Politics in the Twenty-First Century*. London: Routledge.
Lubac, Henri de. 1995. *The Drama of Atheist Humanism*. San Francisco: Ignatius Press.
Luckmann, Thomas. 1967. *The Invisible Religion: The Problem of Religion in Modern Society*. New York: Macmillan.
Luhmann, Niklas. 1977. *Funktion der Religion*. Frankfurt/M.: Suhrkamp.

Macherey, Pierre. 1991. "Le positivisme entre la révolution et la contre-révolution: Comte et Maistre." *Revue de synthèse*, 112:41–47.

de Maistre, Joseph. 1831. *Considérations sur la France* (nouvelle edition). Lyon: Rusand.

de Maistre, Joseph. 850. *The Pope Considered in his Relation with the Church, Temporal Sovereignties, Separated Churches, and the Cause of Civilization* (English transl. by A. McD. Dawson). London: Dolman.

Maurras, Charles. 1978. *La démocratie religieuse*. Paris: Nouvelles Éditions Latines.

Milbank, John. 2006. *Theology and Social Theory. Beyond Secular Reason*[2]. Oxford: Blackwell.

Nisbet, Robert. 2004. *The Sociological Tradition* (sixth printing, with a new introduction by the author). New Brunswick, NJ: Transaction Publishers.

Novalis. 1968 [1799]. *Die Christenheit oder Europa: Ein Fragment*. In *Novalis, Schriften: Die Werke Friedrich von Hardenbergs*, III, Stuttgart: Kohlhammer. 507–525.

Oldfield, John J. 1973. *The Problem of Tolerance and Social Existence in the Writings of Félicité Lamennais, 1809–1831*. Leiden: Brill.

Parsons, Talcott. 1966. "Religion in a Modern Pluralistic Society." *Review of Religious Research*, 7:125–146.

Pew Forum. 2008. "U.S. Religious Landscape Survey: Religious Beliefs and Practices." At: https://www.pewforum.org/2008/06/01/u-s-religious-landscape-survey-religious-beliefs-and-practices/ (accessed February 23, 2020).

Rousseau, Jean-Jacques. 1997. *"The Social Contract" and Other Later Political Writings*, ed. and English transl. by Victor Gourevitch. Cambridge: Cambridge University Press.

Rüpke, Jörg. 2005. "Varro's *Tria Genera Theologiae*: Religious Thinking in the Late Republic." *Ordia Prima*, 4:107–129.

Saint-Simon, Henri de. 1859. *Oeuvres choisies de C.H. de Saint-Simon: Précédées d'un essai sur sa doctrine*. I–III. Brussels: F. van Meeten.

Schmitt, Carl. 1970. *Politische Theologie*, II: *Die Legende von der Erledigung jeder Politischen Theologie*. Berlin: Duncker & Humblot.

Schmitt, Carl. 1979. *Politische Theologie: Vier Kapitel zur Lehre von der Souveränität*. Berlin: Duncker & Humblot.

Spaemann, Robert. 1998 [1959]. *Der Ursprung der Soziologie aus dem Geist der Restauration: Studien über L.G.A. de Bonald*. Stuttgart: Klett-Cotta.

Stroumsa, Guy G. 2010. *A New Science: The Discovery of Religion in the Age of Reason*. Cambridge, MA: Harvard University Press.

Vega, Facundo. 2017. "On the Tragedy of the Modern Condition: The 'Theologico-Political Problem' in Carl Schmitt, Leo Strauss, and Hannah Arendt." *The European Legacy: Towards New Paradigms*, 22:697–782.

Wernick, Andrew. 2004. *Auguste Comte and the Religion of Humanity: The Post-Theistic Program of French Social Theory*. Cambridge, UK: Cambridge University Press.

Zachhuber, Johannes. 2020. "Religion and National Identity in Modern Western Societies: Theological Reflections on a Political Problem." In: Henning Glaser (ed.), *Political and Religious Communities: Partners, Competitors, or Aliens* (CPG Series of Comparative Constitutional Law, Politics and Governance). Baden-Baden: Nomos. Forthcoming.

Jonathan Garb

# The Conversion of the Jews: Identity as Ontology in Modern Kabbalah

## Introduction

One of the uncomfortable, one might even say repressed, chapters in the history of the Kabbalah is the attitude to non-Jews manifested in the majority of texts in this vast literature. Apart from a relatively short Hebrew article by Moshe Hallamish, the first study dedicated to this thorny issue was Elliot Wolfson's *Venturing Beyond: Law and Morality in Kabbalistic Mysticism* (2006).[1] One of the merits of Wolfson's treatment is that it includes an extensive comparison between rabbinic and kabbalistic views of the election of the Jewish people, thus excusing me from entering into this question, which pertains to late antiquity rather than to my field of modernity.[2] Succinctly put, Wolfson's main argument is that the kabbalistic mainstream upheld an ontic divide between Jews and non-Jews, closely related, as we shall soon see, to a similar ontologization of sexual difference, focused on the male body.

As the ontological and the psychological are closely related in kabbalistic discourse, this view leads into the assumption that not just the circumcised male Jewish body, but the Jewish soul is derived from a different order of being than the non-Jewish soul. A prominent example of this is to be found in the thirteenth century classic, the Zohar, which stresses that the souls of non-Jewish nations are derived from the "side of impurity." Therefore, it is only the Jews who are truly created in God's holy image, in a subversion of the plain meaning of Gen. 1:26–27, in which Man as such is described in these terms.[3] To be sure, one can find more philosophically oriented thinkers in this first golden age of Kabbalah, such as R. Abraham Abulafia, who largely resisted such ontic distinctions. As Moshe Idel has shown, Abulafia's views continued to impact more universalistic forms of

1 Hallamish 1998; Wolfson 2006.

2 Likewise, I cannot enter here into the large scholarly literature on views of conversion in biblical, inter-testamental, halakhic, pietistic and philosophical literature, etc. See, e.g., Kellner 2019; Lasker 1990; Porton 1994; Thiessen 2011; and Reiner 2012.

3 Zohar I:131a–b; III:104b, see parallels in Wolfson 2006:49, 81–82.

https://doi.org/10.1515/9783110723984-003

kabbalistic thought, as in the Italian Renaissance.[4] However, these remain exceptions to a general rule.

My own contribution to this debate has been to point to the intensification of the discourse of ontic distinction in the modern period, as part of what I have termed "the nationalization of Kabbalah," itself a response to the hardening of national and confessional identities due to processes of modernization.[5] Here one should mention a similar thesis, that of Shaul Magid, who has interpreted foundational texts in the first major wave of modern kabbalistic discourse, in sixteenth-century Safed, in terms of responses to the return of *conversos* to Judaism and the subsequent problematization of Jewish identity.[6] Looking again at psychology, I have related this process to the modern ascendancy of the model of the divine, prenatal origin of the Jewish soul, displacing earlier models of the soul's gradual acquisition of its various levels in the course of a lifetime and based on one's actions.[7]

The deepening, in modern kabbalistic writing, of the ontic divide between the basic constitutions of Jews and non-Jews sharpens the already latent question of the very possibility of conversion. If a non-Jewish soul is derived from the side of impurity and does not partake of the divine image, how can the rite of conversion, stringent as it may be, bridge this chasm and transform the very being of a non-Jew? Jochanan Wijnhoven began to address this question, albeit in the pre-modern context, in his 1975 article "The Zohar and the Proselyte." Though this early essay doesn't differentiate sufficiently between the various strata of the Zoharic corpus, it cites important texts disclosing a quasi-biological distinction between the "pure seed" and the converts. It also points to a more positive view of the latter in the *Midrash hane'elam* section.[8]

In his far more extensive treatment of the issue, Wolfson has pointed to various resolutions of this quandary. These include the sixteenth-century notion, originating in Safed and in turn based on a talmudic adage, that the Diaspora was devised precisely to collect the "sparks" of souls of divine origin scattered amongst the "thorns" of the nations;[9] an earlier, Zoharic model ascribing a profound transformation of identity to the focal rite of circumcision; and a more

4 Idel 2011:18–21, 29, 157, 218, 337–339. Cf. Wolfson 2000:211–221.

5 See Garb 2013; Weinstein 2011:409–415. On the autonomy of modern Kabbalah in general, see Garb 2016.

6 Magid 2008.

7 Garb 2015.

8 Wijnhoven 1975.

9 See BT *Pesaḥim* 87b, as well as Shapira 1882:12a, and the rather negative formulation of this idea in Weisblum 1866:26a, 62a.

radical view, according to which conversion merely reveals the convert's hidden Jewish identity. One should pause here to note the ensuing question: In the last case why does one really need the rite with all its details? However, Wolfson also uncovered a hostile attitude toward conversion, found in a later stratum of the Zoharic literature (the fourteenth-century *Tikune Zohar*), continuing the talmudic view of R. Ḥelbo: "Converts are as difficult for Israel as a scab" (BT *Yevamot* 47b). The *Tikune Zohar* employs another talmudic statement, according to which converts will not be accepted in the messianic era (BT *Yevamot* 24b, and cf. 13b).[10] This position was upheld and reinforced with further rationales by the Kabbalists of Safed, representing the first major wave of modern Kabbalah, and especially R. Moses Cordovero and R. Isaac Luria.[11]

All of these models are certainly present in modern kabbalistic discussions, yet I wish to point to several other solutions offered to the riddle of conversion, and to the manner in which earlier views were reworked and reinterpreted in the modern context. In doing so, I shall partly follow the geographical trajectory of the Kabbalah of Safed as it spread into central, southern and then eastern Europe, before returning to Erets Israel in the twentieth century.[12]

## Conversion in Central European Kabbalah

My starting point will be the voluminous corpus penned by R. Judah Loew (the Maharal) of Prague (1520?–1609). As I have suggested elsewhere, Judah Loew epitomizes the emergence of modern Kabbalah, both in his national interpretation of earlier texts and in his attempt to translate kabbalistic ideas into non-kabbalistic

---

**10** Wolfson 2006:113–114, 165–174. On the centrality of circumcision in Zoharic thought, see Wolfson 2003. See also Mopsik 2005:69.

**11** Cordovero 1962:13, 3, and cf. Vital 2013, Part 2:116a, and Vital 1972:93a, which is especially interesting as it compares the liminal status of converts, situated in the median realm between the domains of purity and impurity, and the liminal status of Bible translations; according to BT *Megila* 3a, Onkelos, composer of the famous translation of the Penateuch into Aramaic, was a convert. At the same time, the Lurianic corpus at times reveals awareness of the divergence of opinions around converts. In Vital(?) 1912, Part 2:3a, the tanaitic sage Hillel's positive attitude is ascribed to his origin in the aspect of lovingkindness (*Ḥesed*), while the negative approach of his opponent Shamai is ascribed to the latter's connection with the aspect of strict judgment (*Gevura*). On subtle differences between Cordovero and Luria with regard to converts, see Meroz 1988:268–269.

**12** Understanding of the process of the spread of Lurianic Kabbalah in the early modern period has been greatly advanced by Avivi 2008.

language and thus render it accessible to wider circles.[13] As David Sorotzkin has argued at length, differentiation, as in the term *nivdal* or "separate," is the keystone of Judah Loew's political theology (as Sorotzkin explicitly calls it). For Judah Loew, the segregated, exceptional status of the Jews in the early modern period, far from being a sign of their inferiority, points to their superior ontic status, their belonging to a different order of being, one that transcends nature and belongs to the miraculous realm.[14]

Our first text is positioned at the beginning of Judah Loew's treatise *Tiferet Yisrael*, on the superiority of the Torah of Israel (a companion to *Netzah Yisrael*, on the superiority of the Jewish people). After quoting the rabbinic assertion that God offered the Torah to the nations of the world, but they refused to accept it, Judah Loew comments:

> And the intention here is that they do not merit the Torah and the commandments, which are the divine actions and deeds, for their soul is not suitable for this; only Israel [merits them], due to their divine soul, which fits them for the divine actions, that is, the commandments of the Torah. And this itself is according to what the Sages said: "you are called Man and the nations of the world are not called Man" [*Yevamot* 61a].

Judah Loew then moves straight into the paradox of conversion:

> And do not ask: "if so how, can the convert accept the Torah, when he has a psychic quality that is not good?" – This is not a difficulty at all, for as he comes to convert he has an Israelite quality, and on converting he becomes subsidiary to the Israelite nation and like it. And even so they [the Sages] said converts are difficult for Israel like a scab, for the scab's temperament is not good and spoils the flesh that has a good temperament.[15]

Judah Loew is working from the rabbinic parallel between conversion and the acceptance of the Torah at Sinai,[16] the latter a theme that also appears elsewhere in his writing.[17] From this perspective, the convert is joining the Jewish (or Israelite, as Judah Loew tellingly has it) acceptance of the Torah rather than the Gentile rejection. Hence, the need for the ritual of conversion, which is a reenactment of the Sinaitic movement rather than a formal, normative procedure. By this action (and action, or actualization [*pe'ula*], is a central theme in Judah Loew's writing), he

**13** Garb 2004a. See recently Reiner 2015.

**14** Sorotzkin 2011, esp.151–153, 168–173, 201–205. See also Wolfson 2006:116–120.

**15** Loew 1980a:10.

**16** See BT *Shabat* 146a. See however Midrash rabba *Bamidbar* 8:4, which distances converts from the event of Sinai.

**17** See e.g. Loew 1980b, I:235.

exposes an Israelite quality in his psyche.[18] At the same time, Judah Loew is firmly within the tradition of R. Ḥelbo, returning for a moment to premodern sources,[19] in assuming that converts retain the negative psychic constitution of their Gentile origins. Although Judah Loew does not resort explicitly to kabbalistic language, the modern mystical ideology of the divinity of the Jewish soul is clearly present in his formulations.[20]

Judah Loew's "family resemblance" to kabbalistic thought becomes clearer in light of a work that was far more influential at the time (though less so today), *Shene luḥot haberit*, by R. Isaiah Horowitz (1558–1630). The author came from an illustrious rabbinic family in Prague and was roughly contemporaneous with Judah Loew in central Europe. While Judah Loew's writings do not display absorption of the Kabbalah of Safed, Horowitz's writings are permeated with Judeocentric notions derived from the doctrine of Cordovero, and to a lesser extent that of Luria.[21] He writes:

> ... the origin of the souls of Israel is in the internal aspect of the [cosmic] tree, and the nations are on its exterior. So that even if he [the gentile] converts and enters into [the domain of] holiness, he does not go so much into its interiority, which is the Holy of Holies. However, the soul of Ruth was from the interior aspect, only that the Holy One Blessed be He conducted her soul in transit [*derekh ma'avar*] through Moab, for a reason known to Him Blessed Be He, as one who grafts one tree onto another. And this is what is meant by the verse: "thou art come to take refuge" [Ruth 2:12], i.e., your coming was through there [Moab], but not your origin.[22]

---

**18** Compare this with the rather negative Lurianic notion that the convert, though it is a sin to reject him, acquires a holy Jewish soul while retaining his sinful Gentile soul. See Vital 1981:97–100, where it is also stated that the souls of the converts are created through abstinence rather than through intercourse. Vital invokes this principle to explain the initial hostility of R. Akiva, reputedly a descendant of converts, toward the Sages (*ibid.*:105; BT *Sanhedrin* 96b), even though he possessed a "very holy and great soul," unlike that of the usual convert. As Vital saw himself as first and foremost the incarnation of a "soul spark" of R. Akiva, he attributed his seminal emissions, during a nine-month period of impotence, to the "filth" of the convert soul mixed in his psyche (*ibid.*:136–138). On Vital's suffering around his period of impotence, see Idel 1988:81. Here we find the modern connection between sexual anxiety and national identity; see the conclusion, below, and see Chajes 2011:17–18. See also the discussion of Vital's views of national identity and sexuality in Magid 2008:111–195 and the general discussion of the Lurianic doctrine of metempsychosis in Fine 2003:305–339.

**19** See Idel 1995:6–15; cf. Garb 2015:14–16.

**20** See Garb 2015:24–52. On Judah Loew's approach to conversion, see Katz 1961:138–142.

**21** See Garb 2004a:352–358; and cf. Wolfson 1992.

**22** Horowitz 2006, II:303 (7).

This complex text blends organic-botanical imagery, also reminiscent of Paulinian tropes,[23] with biblical exegesis and the theosophical, Lurianic notion of the transit, or the temporary transmission of divine potencies that properly belong to a higher realm via a lower one.[24] In this context, the foundational act of conversion by the matriarch of the Davidic lineage poses a certain dilemma. Ruth did not seem to go through any formal process of conversion; she merely said to another woman (and not the three-person court required by the Talmud): "Thy people shall be my people, and thy God my God" (Ruth 1:16). Horowitz responds explicitly to this dilemma by according Ruth, "the mother of royalty" (*Midrash Ruth zuta* 1), a unique status amongst converts, and assigning the true origin of her soul entirely to the Jewish source. Her Moabite identity is merely a temporary and mysterious ruse.[25]

A highly influential mediator of Lurianic Kabbalah in its move to central Europe was R. Naftali Bacharach's *Emek hamelekh*, printed in the mid-seventeenth century.[26] I shall select but one of several of his discussions of conversion, as it uses the word *geza'*, "trunk" or "stem," in a meaning not far from its additional derivative Modern Hebrew meaning of "race." Here one must delve into the intricacies of the Lurianic system of *partsufim*, or anthropomorphic configurations. Bacharach commences with describing the character, as it were, of the configuration of *ima*, "mother."[27] Although he briefly acknowledges the parental care of *aba*, the paternal configuration, he focuses on *ima*, which fulfills gendered

---

**23** The Paulinian image, obviously moving in the opposite direction of the gentiles being grafted onto the tree and replacing at least some of the Jews, is found in Romans 11:17–24. The image of conversion as grafting is found in a sixteenth-century Safedian treatise by R. Shlomo Turiel (see Scholem 2008:115). On "the organic model" in Kabbalah, see Garb 2004b:282–283 and the earlier studies cited there (especially that of Wolfson 1995:63–88); BT *Kidushin* 40b should be added as an important primary source. On organic imagery in nationalistic thought, see recently Mann 2005, esp. 61–69. An important possible source for Horowitz here is Joseph Gikatilla's *Gates of Light* (Gikatilla 1994:226), a work often quoted by him.

**24** See, e.g., Vital 1981:166. The theosophical and psychological aspects of this theme need to be researched at greater length.

**25** This ruse is probably that of sending the soul of the Messiah via an impure conduit so as to avoid it being intercepted by the forces of impurity, and idea developed especially in the sixteenth-century work *Galia raza*, on which see Elior 1995. Elsewhere, Horowitz (1992, I:251–252) relates converts to demonic activity: The archetypal she-demon Lilith steals Israelite souls at night (as a result of improper sexual activity) and turns them into the souls of converts, who then need to make their way back to the Jewish people.

**26** On this work, see Liebes 1993; Shatil 2010.

**27** The use of the term "character" is deliberate, as it is an important term in nationalistic discourse on "national character." Some important studies of this term, from diverse angles, are Fromm 1963:239–253; Hillman 1999; Hunter 2001; Martindale 1967; and Sennet 2000.

expectations by constant selfless nurturing of the lower *partsufim*, the son and the daughter.[28] Predictably, Bacharach focuses on the relationship between *ima* and her son, utilizing the explicit metaphor of the "woman adorning her son ... and although she gives to him, this is not enough in her eyes, and she ever sees him as needing more refinement [*tikun*]."[29] In a deft move from gender to nationality, Bacharach implicitly asserts that this quality of beneficence is imbibed, as it were, by the son, now representing the Jewish national collective:

> ... and thus Israel are the merciful sons of the merciful,[30] and each of them bestows good on his fellow, for the nature of good is to do good, and they are from the spark of holiness; their soul is from the supernal *ima*. And whoever does not possess this virtue, it is known that his ancestors did not stand at Mount Sinai [*Yevamot* 79a], and they are of the stem (*geza'*) of converts and nations that mixed in Israel, so that he still adheres to the nature of his stem; understand this.[31]

Blending organic imagery with notions of admixture, Bacharach's view of the Jewish national character reflecting gendered, familial processes in the divine realm, in tandem with a negative attitude toward converts, can be seen as a clear instance of nationalistic discourse, written just before the 1648–1649 Chmielnicki pogroms. This tragic event manifested both the rise of national-religious bigotry and its destabilizing effect on Jewish life in the new centers of eastern Europe, eventually leading to the Zionist response, with which we shall conclude.

The latter part of the seventeenth century, coming after what some historians describe as its "general crisis," was largely dominated by the Sabbatean outbreak, which often took root in *converso* circles. Sabbatean thought was dominated by transformation of identity in the opposite direction – the would-be Messiah's conversion to Islam.[32] The next significant ideational development of our theme emerged in the second area to which Lurianic Kabbalah spread from Safed – northern Italy.

---

**28** The literature on Kabbalah and gender is quite large by now and rather mixed in quality. Two foundational works are Mopsik 2005 and Wolfson 2005. For a good summary, see Tirosh-Samuelson 2011.

**29** Bacharach 2003, I:392. On the redemption of the pious of the nations in the eschaton (generally characterized by conquest and vengeance), see II:748–749. For a reworking of an older Ashkenazi tradition of conversion of foes through the magical activity of the righteous (as we shall soon see in the case of R. Naḥman of Bratslav), see II:764.

**30** I have not found this precise phrase earlier than the anonymous fourteenth-century *Sefer haḥinukh*.

**31** Bacharach 2003, I:392.

**32** See at length in Wolfson 2006:176–185; Liebes 1995:20–34.

## Conversion as Alchemy and Theurgy: Moshe David Valle

Here I shall focus on R. Moses David Valle (1697–1777) of Padua, a close associate of the more famous Kabbalist polymath R. Moses Ḥayyim Luzzatto (1707–1746?). Luzzatto has only two major statements on the topic of conversion. One is found in a discussion of Israel and the nations, replete with organic imagery, in which he succinctly states that God's grace (a major theme in his writing) has granted the "branches" of the nations the opportunity to tear themselves from their own roots and be included among the branches of Abraham.[33] The other, found in his major mystical work, *Adir bamarom*, states that in the messianic future, the aspect of Abraham, representing the primal ray of light descending into the space empty of divine light (as explicated in Lurianic Kabbalah), shall rectify all the nations by converting them.[34]

By contrast, Valle refers to this issue (as well as the reverse direction of apostasy) hundreds of times in his voluminous oeuvre, parts of which are extant in manuscripts.[35] One of the more interesting of these statements is found in a marginal note comparing the return of converts to the Jewish people to the alchemical process of transmutation of base metals. Although Valle describes the latter project as a waste of time and money, he nonetheless sees the conversion of copper and iron into silver and gold as an apt image for the restoration of the "lost object."[36] An interesting expression of this idea of conversion as rectification is found in Valle's commentary on Jeremiah, where he ascribes the travails of the prophet to his descent from a woman convert, Rahab, and the consequent need to rectify the evil elements that he inherited.[37]

Similarly to Horowitz, Valle repeatedly emphasizes that in the eschaton the converts will remain in the external and inferior domains of holiness and thus at a remove from the Tree of Life, which is reserved for the Jews as the children of God.[38] In one discussion, he posits that they will inherit the domains of impurity (i.e., of the non-converting nations), which will be destroyed in order to resettle

---

**33** Luzzatto 1977:137 (2:4:4).

**34** Luzzatto 1995:351–353. The clearest exposition of Lurianic theosophy remains Scholem 1941:260–278.

**35** On Valle, see Tishby 2008:289–403; Garb 2010:9–16; Garb 2011.

**36** See Valle 1998, I:214.

**37** Valle 2003:7, 123. I hope to expand elsewhere on Valle's treatment of Jeremiah's psychology. Cf. his interpretation of R. Ḥelbo's saying in terms of the difficulty of removing the evil that clings to converts in Valle 2009:216.

**38** Valle 1999:445–446.

the converts.[39] Furthermore, rather than being a chosen act of reshaping identity, conversion in the messianic period will be an involuntary result of the victory of holiness, the image being that of a manacled slave.[40] However, it appears that Valle has a different attitude toward those who convert in the present, who are worthy of experiencing the divine presence or *Shekhina*.[41] In one place, he even goes so far as to describe conversion as a wondrous change in the "order of creation," like a thorn becoming a rose (a classic symbol of the *Shekhina* in kabbalistic writing).[42] In an explicit theoretical reflection on the boundaries between holiness and the "husks" (the standard kabbalistic image for forces of impurity), he compares the ability of converts to cross this boundary to the activity of the "winnower" (none other than himself, as previous scholarly writing has shown), crossing this border on a similar theurgical mission of sifting sparks of holiness from amongst the husks.[43]

## Hasidic Views

Moving now to the Hasidic movement, which emerged in eastern Europe toward the end of Valle's long life, I shall focus on the varied and ultimately positive views of converts found in the writings of R. Naḥman of Bratslav (1772–1810). R. Naḥman starkly poses our central question: "But how can one make converts, as they are very distant from the holiness of Israel, and whence comes the understanding that leads them to convert?" Typically, his response employs images of communication: a letter sent to a distant destination, or a sound conveyed over long distances if the air is pure and the weather calm. Combining these images, R. Naḥman asserts that holy speech spoken in pure and calm air reaches the Gentiles and is written in their languages and books, challenging the existing beliefs of potential converts and setting off their quest. "We have found some converts who converted because of this," he writes.[44] This text may justifiably be read as a reference to the subtle circulation of Jewish ideas undermining Christian certainties in the modern period. Elsewhere, R. Naḥman goes so far as to remark that some gentiles can remain "potential" converts "in their place," as their previous

39 Valle 1999:55. I hope to discuss elsewhere Valle's general approach to the future of the nations (destruction being but one of three models).
40 Valle 1999:378.
41 See Valle 2008:, I:101; II:101; cf.II:376.
42 Valle 1995, I:223.
43 Valle 2009:127.
44 Nahman of Bratslav 1994, I:17:5.

beliefs weaken and they adopt true, monotheistic (presumably, as opposed to Trinitarian) beliefs.[45]

Thus, displaying a strikingly positive attitude, R. Naḥman depicts converts as individuals with a strong sense of intellectual honesty, influenced by the remote effects of the work of the *tsadikim*, the righteous (the main subject of this text and many others). They reveal the divine glory, eventually leading to the spread of prophecy amongst the Jews.[46] In other words, conversion has a reciprocal effect on the Jews and their mystics. R. Naḥman here is reworking notions that originated in Safed regarding the sexual activity of the righteous and the "unifications" performed through their prayer as creating the souls of converts.[47] While some Hasidic masters, such as R. Moses Ḥayyim Ephraim of Sudylkow (c. 1740–1800), cite the Baal Shem Tov (the founder of Hasidism, of whom both he and R. Naḥman were direct descendants) as ascribing this activity to a state of "smallness," one cannot find such reservations in R. Naḥman's texts.[48] Rather, R. Naḥman writes that the "intercourse of souls" gives birth to the souls of the righteous.[49] Of course, he does not ignore R. Ḥelbo, but he transfers responsibility for the negative effects of conversion to his rabbinic opponents: By increasing beliefs close to Judaism, the converts restore the Jewish pride absent in exile, but this pride is abused by "the leaders of the generation," who are actually the converts referred to by R. Ḥelbo.[50] This interpretation, typical of R. Naḥman's hermeneutical virtuosity, is an astounding reversal of the original intent of the talmudic saying.[51]

It is interesting to compare R. Naḥman's views with those of another highly original writer, R. Mordecai Joseph Leiner of Izbica (1800–1854). For Leiner, the convert with clear intention of the heart is named righteous (*ger tsedek*), while the deeds of those whose sincerity is not "clarified" are nothing. They differ in this

---

**45** *Ibid.*, II:5:4.

**46** *Ibid.*, II:8:4–5.

**47** Cordovero 1962, Part 2:76b. It is interesting that this activity of the righteous serves as a form of procreation for infertile or unmarried figures: See Vital 1981:98–99. Cf. Vital n.d. [1804]:14a, on the intercourse of the righteous as pure pleasure that is dedicated to the excess or surplus production of souls of converts.

**48** See Moshe Ḥayyim Ephraim of Sudylkow 1810:10a (recording a tradition in the name of R. Dov Baer of Mezeritch) and the fascinating sexual imagery found there. On the state of smallness in Hasidic psychology, see Pachter 2004:185–234.

**49** Naḥman of Bratslav 1994, I:14: 4; and cf. II:8:12. See also Twersky 2008:299 (and 127).

**50** Naḥman of Bratslav 1994, II:5:5.

**51** The positive attitude toward converts continues amongst prominent contemporary representatives of his school. See Morgenstern 2015:245, according to whom on one level the souls of converts are even higher than those of Jews!

from born Jews, "the seed of Israel," whose deeds are clarified by God, at times retroactively, to be sincere at their root and in the depths of their hearts, even if their intention is not.[52] While Leiner retains the usual sense of national distinction and thus sets a higher bar for converts, R, Nahman blames any failure in their reception on the rabbinic leadership.

## The Twentieth Century

My title, "The Conversion of the Jews," is derived from the eponymous, controversial short story in Philip Roth's debut book, *Goodbye, Columbus, and Five Short Stories* (1959). As Shaul Magid has shown in *American Post-Judaism: Identity and Renewal in a Post-Ethnic Society* (2013), some recent American Jewish mystical thinkers, such as the late R. Zalman Schachter-Shalomi, have sought to undermine concrete and reified notions of Jewish election and distinction, to the extent of questioning the very need for non-Jews seeking (for familial or other reasons) a connection to Judaism to undergo the conversion rite.[53] As Magid has shown, the sociogenesis of such views includes, but is not limited to, the prevalence in the American Jewish milieu of marriage to non-Jewish spouses, often accompanied by forms of conversion that do not require abandoning one's former ethnic identity.[54] This is the same challenge that led the Halabi (Aleppan) Syrian community in New York to issue a *takana* (edict) in 1935 (reaffirmed in 2006) prohibiting marriage to converts.[55]

More generally, Schachter-Shalomi's Jewish Renewal movement, and other forms of Jewish mysticism loosely affiliated with the New Age, contrast with the general tendency in twentieth-century Kabbalah toward accentuating nationalist psychology, as can be seen especially among the followers of R. Abraham Isaac Hakohen Kook (1865–1935) in Israel, where we find explicit positive references to *Völkerpsychologie*.[56] Just recently (August 2015), dozens of leading rabbis from

---

**52** Leiner 1995, II:47. Retroactive clarification of Jewish deeds lies at the core of Leiner's unique system. Of several verses referring the "seed of Israel," it seems that Leiner has Isaiah 45:25 in mind.

**53** R. Nahman's notion of 'potential conversion' is less radical than but resonates with Schachter-Shalomi's ideas.

**54** Magid 2013:48–56.

**55** Thus, I must take issue with Magid's cautious suggestion that Habad is perhaps the least encouraging of conversion amongst ultra-Orthodox American groups.

**56** See Garb 2009:141, note 23; idem 2015:91–92, and the Hebrew studies cited there. On Jewish Renewal in Israel see Werczberger 2016.

this school, most prominently R. Tsvi Israel Tau, signed a petition against private conversions (aimed at bypassing the stringent approach of the Rabbinate), which they describe as undermining the Jewish identity of the state of Israel, and thus its very foundations.[57] It is not entirely clear that R. Kook himself espoused such views; in one early text, he writes of the blessing brought to the people of Israel by "the excellent amongst converts," as an example of the possibility of recasting shared human interiority in the unique and pure Jewish form.[58]

## Conclusion

Our brief and far from exhaustive survey of attitudes toward conversion in modern Kabbalah points to their role in the formation of Jewish national identity, peaking in the R. Kook circle, whose dominance in Israeli society (though far less in the Diaspora) is constantly increasing. In particular, one sees that Wolfson's conclusions are borne out in the many texts (such as those of Bacharach) that point to the strong connection between nationalism and gender exposed by studies such as those of George Mosse. However, this is not a constant, as shown by the case of Judah Loew. Apart from sexuality, "national" mysticism intersects with a variety of concepts, such as the organic imagery used by Horowitz, again well known from general studies of nationalism, and the early modern interest in alchemy, also reflected in the imagery favored by R. Moses David Valle.

The strong presence of nationalistic discourse in modern kabbalistic discussions of conversion does not always entail a negative attitude, as we have seen in the case of R. Naḥman of Bratslav (and to a lesser extent in Luzzatto's vision of universal conversion). One might also ask whether we are dealing with theoretical discussions or reflections of encounters with actual converts, as in the case of one strikingly positive formulation, by the renowned Moroccan kabbalistic writer R. Ḥayyim ben 'Attar (1696–1743): "Go and learn how several of the great of the world come from the nations ... and as we have seen with our own eyes converts that come to convert of their own accord."[59] It is the repeated intersection of such

57 The petition can be viewed at http://goo.gl/ebkrJw (accessed May 19, 2019). The Kook circle consciously continues the twelfth-century views of R. Judah Halevy, who, in the *Kuzari*, insists on the lesser status of converts, as part of his doctrine of the quasi-genetic "divine matter" transmitted with the Jewish ethnos. Judah Loew is another major influence on this school. On Judah Loew and Halevy, see Sorotzkin 2011:174–177. On Tau and national mystical psychology, see Garb 2015:101–102.

58 Kook 1967.

59 Ḥayyim Ben 'Attar, *Or haḥayyim* on Deut. 21:11–14.

concerns that makes up the intricate mosaic that I have conceptualized, in a series of studies, as modern Kabbalah.

## References

Avivi Yosef. 2008. *Kabbala Luriana*. Jerusalem: Yad Ben Zvi. I–III (Hebrew).

Bacharach, Naftali. 2003 [1648]. *Emek hamelekh*. Jerusalem: Yerid Hasefarim. I–II.

Chajes, J.H. 2011. *Between Worlds: Dybbuks, Exorcists, and Early Modern Judaism*. Philadelphia: University of Pennsylvania Press.

Cordovero, Moses. 1962 [1548]. *Pardes rimonim*. Jerusalem: Yeshivat haḥayyim vehashalom.

Elior, Rachel. 1995. "The Doctrine of Transmigration in 'Galya raza.'" In: Lawrence Fine (ed.), *Essential Papers on Kabbalah*. New York: New York University Press. 243–269.

Fine, Lawrence. 2003. *Physician of the Soul, Healer of the Cosmos: Itzhak Luria and his Kabbalistic Fellowship*. Stanford: Stanford University Press.

Fromm, Erich. 2003. *The Fear of Freedom*. London: Routledge and Kegan Paul.

Garb, Jonathan. 2004a. "On The Kabbalists of Prague." *Kabbalah*, 14:347–383 (Hebrew).

Garb, Jonathan. 2004b. *Manifestations of Power in Jewish Mysticism from Rabbinic Literature to Safedian Kabbalah*. Jerusalem: Magnes Press (Hebrew).

Garb, Jonathan. 2009. *The Chosen Will Become Herds: Studies in Twentieth-Century Kabbalah* (English transl. by Y. Berkovits-Murciano). New Haven, CT: Yale University Press.

Garb, Jonathan. 2010. "The Modernization of Kabbalah: A Case Study." *Modern Judaism*, 30:1–22.

Garb, Jonathan. 2011. "A Renewed Study of the Self-Image of R. Moshe David Valle, as Reflected in His Biblical Exegesis." *Tarbiz*, 69:265–306 (Hebrew).

Garb, Jonathan. 2013 "The Psychological Turn in Sixteenth-Century Kabbalah." In: G. Cecere, M. Loubet and S. Pagani (eds.), *Mystique juives, chrétiennes et musulmanes dans L'Egypte médiévale (VIIe–XVIe siècle): Interculturalités et contextes historiques*. Cairo: IFAO. 109–124.

Garb, Jonathan. 2015. *Yearnings of the Soul: Psychological Thought in Modern Kabbalah*. Chicago: University of Chicago Press.

Garb, Jonathan. 2016. *Modern Kabbalah as an Autonomous Domain of Research*. Los Angeles: Cherub Press.

Gikatilla, Joseph. 1994 [13th cent.]. *Sha'are Orah: The Gates of Light* (English transl. by A. Weinstein). San Francisco: Harper Collins.

Hallamish, Moshe. 1998. "The Relation to the Nations of the World in the World of the Kabbalists." *Jerusalem Studies in Jewish Thought*, 14:49–71 (Hebrew).

Hillman, James. 1999. *The Force of Character and the Lasting Life*. New York: Random House.

Hunter, James D. 2001. *The Death of Character: Moral Education in an Age without Good and Evil*. New York: Basic Books.

Horowitz, Isaiah. 1992 [1648]. *Shney Luchot Habrit on the Written Torah by Rabbi I.H. Horowitz* (English transl. by Eliyahu Munk). Jerusalem. I–III.

Horowitz, Isaiah. 2006 [1648]. *Shene luḥot haberit hashalem*. Haifa: Yad Rama. I–III.

Idel, Moshe. 1988. *Kabbalah: New Perspectives*. New Haven, CT: Yale University Press.

Idel, Moshe. 1995. *Hasidism: Between Ecstasy and Magic*. Albany: State University of New York Press.

Idel, Moshe. 2011. *Kabbalah in Italy, 1280–1510*. New Haven, CT: Yale University Press.

Katz, Jacob. 1961. *Exclusiveness and Tolerance: Studies in Jewish-Gentile Relations in Medieval and Modern Times*. Oxford: Oxford University Press.

Kellner, Menachem. 2019. "Converts – The Most Jewish of Jews." *Jewish Thought*, 1:33–52.

Kook, Abraham Isaac. 1967. *Eder hayekar ve'ikve hatson*. Jerusalem: Mossad Harav Kook.

Lasker, Daniel. 1990. "Proselyte Judaism, Christianity, and Islam in the Thought of Judah Halevi." *Jewish Quarterly Review*, 81:75–91.

Leiner, Mordecai J. 1995 [1860]. *Mey hashiloaḥ*. Bene Berak: Institute for the Publication of Izbica-Radzin Writings. I–II.

Liebes, Yehuda. 1993. "Toward a Study of the Author of Emek hamelekh: His Personality, Writings and Kabbalah." *Jerusalem Studies in Jewish Thought*, 11:101–137 (Hebrew).

Liebes, Yehuda. 1995. *On Sabbateaism and Its Kabbalah: Collected Essays*. Jerusalem: Bialik Institute (Hebrew).

Loew, Judah. 1980a [1599]. *Tiferet Yisrael*. Bene Berak.

Loew, Judah. 1980b [1578]. *Gur arye*. Bene Berak. I–V.

Luzzatto, Moses Ḥayyim. 1977 [c. 1740]. *Derech haShem: The Way of God* (English transl. by A. Kaplan). New York–Jerusalem: Feldheim.

Luzzatto, Moses Ḥayyim. 1995 [18th cent.]. *Adir bamarom hashalem*, ed. J. Spinner. Jerusalem.

Magid, Shaul. 2008. *From Metaphysics to Midrash: Myth, History, and the Interpretation of Scripture in Lurianic Kabbala*. Bloomington: Indiana University Press.

Magid, Shaul. 2013. *American Post-Judaism: Identity and Renewal in a Postethnic Society*. Bloomington: Indiana University Press.

Mann, Michael. 2005. *The Dark Side of Democracy: Explaining Ethnic Cleansing*. Cambridge University Press.

Martindale, Don. 1967. "The Sociology of National Character." *Annals of the American Academy of Political and Social Studies*, 370:30–35.

Meroz, Ronit. 1988. "The Teachings of Redemption in Lurianic Kabbalah." Ph.D. Dissertation, The Hebrew University of Jerusalem (Hebrew).

Mopsik, Charles. 2005. *Sex of the Soul: The Vicissitudes of Sexual Difference in Kabbalah*, ed. Daniel Abrams. Los Angeles: Cherub Press.

Morgenstern, Isaac Meir. 2015. *She'erit Yaakov on Tractate Berakhot*. Jerusalem: Makhon Yam haḥokhma.

Moses Ḥayyim Ephraim of Sudylkow. 1810. *Degel maḥane Efrayim*. Koretz.

Naḥman of Bratslav 1994 [1808]. *Likute moharan*. Jerusalem: Bratslav Hasidim Foundation.

Pachter, Mordechai. 2004. *Roots of Faith and Devequt: Studies in the History of Kabbalistic Ideas*. Los Angeles: Cherub Press.

Porton, Gary G. 1994. *The Stranger within Your Gates: Converts and Conversion in Rabbinic Literature*. Chicago: University of Chicago Press.

Reiner, Avraham (Rami). 2012. "On the Attitude toward Converts in Ashkenaz and France in the Eleventh–Thirteenth Centuries." In: idem et al. (eds.), *Ta Shma: Studies in Judaica in Memory of Israel M. Ta-Shma*, II. Alon Shevut: Tevunot Press. 747–769 (Hebrew).

Reiner, Elchanan (ed.). 2015. *Maharal – Overtures: Biography, Doctrine, Influence*. Jerusalem: Zalman Shazar Center (Hebrew).

Scholem, Gershom G. 1941. *Major Trends in Jewish Mysticism*. New York: Schocken.

Scholem, Gershom G. 2008. *Lurianic Kabbalah: Collected Studies by Gershom Scholem*, ed. D. Abrams. Los Angeles: Cherub (Hebrew).

Sennet, Richard. 2000. *The Corrosion of Character: The Personal Consequences of Work*. New York: Norton.

Shatil, Sharron. 2010. "The Doctrine of Secrets of Emeq ha-Melech." *Jewish Studies Quarterly*, 17:358–395.
Shapira, Nathan Neta. 1882. *Megale 'amukot*. Lemberg.
Sorotzkin, David. 2011. *Orthodoxy and Modern Disciplination: The Production of the Jewish Tradition in Modern Times*. Tel Aviv: Hakibbutz hameuchad (Hebrew).
Thiessen, Matthew. 2011. *Contesting Conversion: Genealogy, Circumcision and Identity in Ancient Judaism and Christianity*. New York: Oxford University Press.
Tirosh-Samuelson, Hava. 2011. "Gender in Jewish Mysticism." In: F.E. Greenspahn (ed.), *Jewish Mysticism and Kabbalah: New Insights and Scholarship*. New York: New York University Press. 191–230.
Tishby, Isaiah. 2008. *Messianic Mysticism: Moshe Hayyim Luzzatto and the Padua School* (English transl. by M. Hoffman). Oxford–Portland: Littman Library of Jewish Civilization.
Twersky, Menahem Nahum. 2008 [1798]. *Ma'or 'enayim*. Ashdod.
Valle, Moses David. 1995 [18th cent.]. *Berit 'olam: Bi'ur sefer Shemot*, ed. J. Spinner. Jerusalem. I–II.
Valle, Moses David. 1998 [18th cent.]. *Sefer halikutim*, ed. J. Spinner. Jerusalem. I–II.
Valle, Moses David. 1999 [18th cent.]. *Teshu'at 'olamim: Bi'ur sefer Yesha'yah*, ed. J. Spinner. Jerusalem.
Valle, Moses David. 2003 [18th cent.]. *Marpe' lashon: Bi'ur sefer Yirmiyahu*, ed. J. Spinner. Jerusalem.
Valle, Moses David. 2008 [18th cent.]. *Bi'ur sefer Tehilim*, ed. J. Spinner. Jerusalem. I–II.
Valle, Moses David. 2009 [18th cent.]. *Bi'ur Trei 'Asar 'al derekh hapardes*, ed. J. Spinner. Jerusalem.
Vital, Hayyim. n.d. [late 16th/early 17th cent.]. *Pri 'etz ḥayim*. Jerusalem [reprint of Dubrovna 1804].
Vital(?), Hayyim. 1912 [late 16th/early 17th cent.]. *Sefer halikutim* (with *She'ar hapesukim*). Jerusalem.
Vital, Hayyim. 1972 [late 16th/early 17th cent.]. *Ta'ame hamitsvot* (with *Likute Torah*). Jerusalem [reprint of Vilna 1880].
Vital, Hayyim. 1981 [late 16th/early 17th cent.]. *Sha'ar hagilgulim*. Jerusalem: Or Ḥozer Yeshiva.
Vital, Hayyim. 2013 [late 16th/early 17th cent.]. *'Etz ḥayim*. Jerusalem: Yerid hasefarim.
Weinstein, Roni. 2011. *Kabbalah and Jewish Modernity*. Tel Aviv: Tel Aviv University Press (Hebrew).
Weisblum, Elimelekh [= Elimelekh of Lyzhansk]. 1866 [1787]. *No'am Elimelekh*. Lvov.
Werczberger, Rachel, 2016. *Jews in the Age of Authenticity: Jewish Spiritual Renewal in Israel*. New York: Peter Lang.
Wijnhoven, Jochanan H.A. 1975. "The Zohar and the Proselyte." In: Michael A. Fishbane and Paul R. Flohr (eds.), *Texts and Responses: Studies Presented to Nahum N. Glatzer on the Occasion of his Seventieth Birthday*. Leiden: Brill. 120–140.
Wolfson, Elliot. 1992. "The Influence of Luria on the Shelah." *Jerusalem Studies in Jewish Thought*, 10:423–458.
Wolfson, Elliot. 1995. *Along the Path: Studies in Kabbalistic Myth, Symbolism, and Hermeneutics*. Albany: State University of New York Press.
Wolfson, Elliot. 2000. *Abraham Abulafia, Kabbalist and Prophet: Hermeneutics, Theosophy, and Theurgy*. Los Angeles: Cherub Press.
Wolfson, Elliot. 2003. "Circumcision, Secrecy, and the Veiling of the Veil: Phallomorphic Exposure and Kabbalistic Esotericism." In: E.W. Mark (ed.), *The Covenant of Circumcision:*

*New Perspectives on an Ancient Jewish Rite*. Hanover–London: Brandeis University Press, 2003. 58–70.

Wolfson, Elliot. 2005. *Language, Eros, Being: Kabbalistic Hermeneutics and Poetic Imagination*. New York: Fordham University Press.

Wolfson, Elliot. 2006. *Venturing Beyond: Law and Morality in Kabbalistic Mysticism*. New York: Oxford University Press.

Rivka Feldhay

# Catholic Europe and Sixteenth-Century Science: A Path to Modernity?

## Problematizing Religion and Modernity

In its twenty-fifth session, in 1563, the Council of Trent decided upon a reform of the Catholic prayer book. The decision entailed correction of the Julian calendar in order to overcome the drift in the date of Easter that had resulted from the inaccurate calculation of the length of the year. According to historian J. North, Luther thought that calendars had nothing to do with faith.[1] But for Catholics, the problem of the calendar did not disappear from view after Trent. In 1582 Pope Gregory XIII (1502–1585) published a papal bull promulgating the reformed calendar that was subsequently to bear his name: the Gregorian calendar.[2] The reform was the product of ten years' work by a committee appointed by the Pope, which included three prominent prelates, an expert on Arabic language and culture, experts in canon law and church history, and three mathematicians[3] who used the astronomical tables calculated on the basis of Copernicus's *De revolutionibus orbium coelestium*. The committee was headed by the Jesuit mathematician Christoph Clavius,[4] the man responsible more than anyone else for instituting a program of mathematical studies into the curriculum of all Jesuit universities, which were among the finest centers of mathematical study in Europe in the sixteenth–seventeenth centuries.

The story of the Gregorian reform throws light on the configuration of religion, knowledge and the state in the Catholic world of the sixteenth century. The state that initiated the reform was a monarchy headed by the Pope, who did not, however, concede his universalistic claims to authority.[5] The papal sovereign had at his disposal the elaborate educational system of the Jesuits, bonded to the papacy by a vow of obedience. The story of the calendar reform exemplifies how and where knowledge, relevant to the state as well as to faith, was produced and diffused. Nevertheless, modern historiography has tended to interpret this complex

1 North 1983:101.
2 Ziggelaar 1983:201–239.
3 Baldini 1983:137–138.
4 Clavius 1603.
5 Prodi 1982; Prodi 2000.

https://doi.org/10.1515/9783110723984-004

configuration in terms, on the one hand, of a struggle between the religious establishment and the secular political authority for hegemonic power, and, on the other, of the subordination of science to the needs of religion. Giordano Bruno's burning at the stake, the ban on Copernicanism and the condemnation of Galileo's *Dialogue* have all been interpreted as hard-core evidence of this conflictual thesis.[6] Concomitantly, Luther's challenge to the ancient bond between knowledge and faith, along with the "Protestant ethic," which encouraged a pragmatic, this-worldly attitude to nature, have been seen as an emancipating path to modernity, leading to the ideal of the autonomy of empirical science in Western culture.[7]

My paper proposes a different approach to such conflictual-emancipatory theses. Rather than describing religious responses to modernity, I shall try to show how Catholicism in the sixteenth–seventeenth centuries *took part in the creation of early modernity*. Following in the footsteps of historian Wolfgang Reinhard,[8] I shall argue that the reconstitution of Christian religious communities after the Protestant/Catholic reformation and the religious wars was performed not simply *against* but rather *in the bosom of* the newly emerging sovereign states, and in association with new types of scientific and artistic practice, equally relevant – albeit in different ways – to the state and to religion. In analyzing the reconfiguration of state–religion–knowledge relationships circa 1550–1650, I shall thus delineate, in very broad lines, the Catholic path to modernity, not in terms of conflict and differentiation from science and the state, but rather in terms of the mutual power consolidation of a common framework.

I shall begin with a short explication of how I use the concepts of modernity, science, religion and the sovereign state in the sixteenth-century context. I shall then briefly delineate the broad constellation in which the arts and sciences, on the one hand, and religion, on the other, were embedded in the realities of the early modern sovereign state. Finally, using one particular example from the Catholic context – the Jesuits and their involvement in state affairs and in the field of the mechanical arts and sciences – I shall argue that Catholic culture, rather than being a hindrance to modernity, offered its own form of being modern, the nature of which will become clearer as we go along.

---

**6** Shea 1986:114–135; Blackwell 1998:348–366.
**7** Merton 1970; Hooykaas 1972.
**8** Reinhard 1977; Reinhard 1989.

## Early Modernity: Science, Religion, State

In speaking of modernity, I follow the late S.N. Eisenstadt, who used to speak of "multiple modernities" as a correction to classic sociological theories of modernization.[9] Marx, Durkheim and Weber posited a coherent, linear process in all societies leading to a Western model of modernity. In their theories, modernity was perceived mainly in terms of political, intellectual and religious progress, articulated in the concepts of sovereignty, the autonomy of science and the confinement of religion to the private sphere. The process of modernity, according to this conception, resulted in a functional differentiation that eventually culminated in the separation of state, science and religion. Many elements of this model were associated with the rise of Protestantism, its challenge to the universal authority of the Pope, the disentanglement of the bond between knowledge and faith, and the privatization of faith, which meant its separation from the state. Eisenstadt, by contrast, insisted on modernization as a process ridden with antinomies, which could lead to enlightenment, democracy and secularization but could also manifest revolutionary violence, terrorism and colonial domination.

I wish to argue that early modernity in Europe indeed offered more than just one path to modernity. By focusing on the Catholic path rather than the Protestant one, I shall describe this "traditional modernity" less in terms of functional differentiation and boundary-making than by focusing on the awareness of the limits of power growing out of *the set of dependencies* between knowledge, religion and the state, enhanced by the paradoxical structure of sovereignty. Simultaneously, I shall show how religion, the arts and the sciences could and did flourish while maintaining their traditions and creating bridges for themselves to the new political entity of the sovereign state.

The terms "science" and "religion" are also in need of explication. First, it should be clear that no "modern science" with a capital S – Science as we think of it today – existed before the nineteenth century.[10] This is a question not only of contents but also of the *institutions and practices* of knowledge production, accumulation and transmission. In contemporary historiography, "science" in the sixteenth century refers mainly to the mathematical disciplines – arithmetic, geometry, astronomy, optics, mechanics and music – as well as the "mechanical arts" – architecture, fortification, geology, agriculture, painting and sculpture.[11]

---

**9** Eisenstadt 2000:1–2.

**10** "The Companion divides modern science into three subperiods. The first and longest, the *Classical Science*, 1830-1915…" Heilbron 2003:372.

**11** Laird and Roux 2008.

All of these "disciplines," with their different mathematical-practical bodies of knowledge, barely featured in medieval university curricula, and even if they were taught, they remained extremely marginal.

As for "religion," according to Wilfred Cantwell Smith, the Latin word *religio* – referring to an aggregation of customs related to various divine entities and expressing fear or reverence of the gods, as well as a set of beliefs – almost disappeared from use between the fifth and fifteenth centuries.[12] In the Middle Ages, the word was used mainly to denote the *religiones*, the different religious orders. Instead, from the fifth century on, *fides* – originally connoting trust and confidence between people – was introduced by the early Christians into the discourse on God and the practices of serving Him.[13] From around the fifteenth century, however, the word "religion" returned to use, with new and additional meanings. It began to refer more to a system – an institutional structure embedded in a set of ideas and enriched with a new discourse on identities.

Finally, the "sovereign state" was a new type of political entity born out of the political and religious upheavals of the long sixteenth century.[14] The emergence of the sovereign state not only signaled the collapse of the medieval, universalistic regimes of the Christian papacy and empire. It also completely changed the meaning of "the political" by making possible a distinction between rulers and the forms of power invested in them, on the one hand, and a "state" common to the people living within recognized territorial boundaries, on the other.[15] I believe the effect of this new phenomenon has not sufficiently been studied in the context of the conversation on religion and modernity.

## The Constellation of the Sovereign State and Its System of Dependencies

Jean Bodin, in *Les six Livres de la Republique* (1576), was probably the first modern to ask what a state is and how it operates.[16] His writings testify to the emergence of a new field of interactions of knowledge, religion and state that will serve as a pivotal point for my argument about early modernity. The unique, unshared and unlimited power of the sovereign first emerges in Bodin's description of the

**12** Smith 1991, Ch. 2.

**13** Smith 1979, Ch. 5.

**14** Hent and Skinner 2010.

**15** Ophir 2010.

**16** Bodin 1967.

King's rule as "absolute" and "perpetuate." The sovereign is characterized as the law-maker: "A law proceeds from him who has sovereign power, and by it he binds the subject to obedience, but cannot bind himself."[17] This is the essence of "absolute" rule. Before Bodin's articulation, God was conceived as the source of all laws pertaining to man and nature.[18] God was the legislator, and human beings – kings, estates, jurists, scholars – had "to find," "to discover," to study and to apply His law.[19] God was also free either to abide by his law – his *potentia ordinata* – or not, in which case he was applying his *potentia absoluta*. But Bodin directly attributed "absolute power" to the Sovereign, a human being assuming analogically unbounded Godly power.

And yet, any effort on the part of historians to understand the phenomenon of the sovereign state in terms of "all power is conveyed to him and vested in him" would be insufficient. While the notion of sovereignty indeed entails the attribution of non-human omnipotence to the ruler, it also creates a new field of duties and obligations between ruler and subjects, structured by the need to *mediate* the huge gap opened up between them. Indeed, Bodin himself goes on to write: "besides sovereign power there must also be something enjoyed in common ... there is no commonwealth where there is no common interest."[20] Here we find the newly defined space common to both sovereign and subjects. In principle, it is a space governed according to the same hierarchical pattern of relationships between ruler and ruled, granting the first the right to receive obedience and imposing on the second the duty to obey. Yet the sovereign's law does not exhaust this relationship, for "the absolute power of princes and sovereign lords *does not* extend to the laws of God and of nature,"[21] and, furthermore, "a law and a covenant must ... not be confused."[22] A covenant, as defined by Bodin, is "a mutual undertaking between a prince and his subjects, *equally binding on both parties*, and neither can contravene it to the prejudice of the other, without his consent. The prince *has no greater privilege* than the subject in this matter."[23] All sorts of covenants regulate public and private life in relation to the ruler.

Contrary to what is perhaps the more common reading of Bodin, the political structure delineated in his text is precariously located between divine omnipotence and human fragility, revealing a desperate need for order and security and

---

**17** Bodin 1967: Book I, Ch. viii.
**18** Elshtain 2008.
**19** Grimm 2015:17–23.
**20** Bodin 1967, Book I, Ch. ii–v.
**21** Bodin 1967, Book I, Ch.viii. My emphasis – R.F.
**22** *Ibid.*
**23** *Ibid.*

also demonstrating the difficulty of attaining them in the here and now. It is thus marked by paradoxes and ambivalences. This situation enhanced the differentiation between spheres of culture – such as science, religion and state – while producing a new network of dependencies between the ruler and various specialists or professionals, including artists, painters and sculptors, who were capable of providing representations to glorify princes and kings, and scientists/engineers, who bore mechanical knowledge relevant for augmenting the ruler's physical force through the military and the economy. It also entailed a religious discourse that became a source of political legitimacy and collective identity.

## The Mechanical Arts and Sciences

Before saying more about the new field of dependencies woven between the mechanical arts and sciences, religion and the emerging sovereign state, and before turning to my concrete example of how this was manifested in the Jesuit colleges, I would like to say a few words about how we should understand the status of the mechanical arts and sciences in that period.

Traditional historiography of the scientific revolution posited the "classical mechanics" of Galileo, Descartes, Kepler and Newton as a coherent, emerging body of knowledge that constituted the core of modern science in the sixteenth–seventeenth centuries. The very notion of a "scientific revolution" assumed that the new mathematical and experimental sciences represented a radical break with the antecedent Aristotelian framework, and that they subsequently gained disciplinary autonomy. However, a historiographical turn in the last twenty years has inspired the study of a variety of discourses on mechanics that existed already in antiquity and late antiquity, were partly revived during the Middle Ages and proliferated rapidly in early modernity.[24] One version of mechanical knowledge, to which I shall refer as "pre-classical mechanics," and in which I include the contributions of Galileo, Kepler and Descartes, gained a certain hegemony circa 1550–1650. In the era from which it emerged, spanning from antiquity to early modernity, theoretical knowledge about mechanical phenomena emerged out of everyday experiences. Its development involved the accumulation of practical know-how concerning tools and machines, accompanied by reflection and subsequent conceptualization of intuitive explanations of the relevant phenomena.[25]

24 Meli 2006; Laird & Roux 2008.
25 Renn and McLaughlin 2018.

From this long-term perspective, pre-classical mechanics can be seen as yet another transformation of old bodies of knowledge enriched by emerging technological innovations, new practices and discourses, and a fruitful encounter between ancient intellectual traditions and new knowledge-sites. It included the study of a variety of natural and artificial phenomena, such as free fall, percussion and oscillation, using concepts such as center of gravity, local motion, acceleration and early formulations of the concepts of momentum. Pre-classical mechanics used heterogeneous resources such as Aristotelian natural philosophy, Archimedean statics, and sophisticated logical and mathematical skills developed within the medieval tradition of the *calculatores*. It is in this framework that Galileo's new theory of motion, for example, took shape, in a broad context that incorporated cosmological and astronomical issues as well as a theory of matter. A final feature of pre-classical mechanics is revealed in the efforts invested by its bearers in incorporating practical knowledge associated with contemporary mechanical technologies relating to such matters as the motion of a pendulum or the trajectory of cannonballs, and in engaging with questions about the very meaning of weight and force in machines and other constructions.

Pre-classical mechanics was first carried by a new class of engineer-scientists, many of them Italian.[26] It was diffused in various sites of knowledge around Europe and beyond, including building sites, workshops and arsenals, universities, Jesuit colleges, academies and courts. Some of these – such as the universities – were traditional centers of knowledge-production and diffusion, which nonetheless underwent transformations in the early modern era.[27] Others, such as the academies, were new types of loose, incoherent institutional structures.[28] Yet others, such as the court or the arsenal, which for the most part were not conceived as sites of knowledge at all by traditional historiographies of science, have come to assume importance in more recent studies.[29]

Most of these new knowledge-sites existed under the patronage of sovereign rulers. Even old universities, such as the university of Pisa, became state universities, losing many of the traditional privileges that had previously guaranteed them some degree of autonomy. Pre-classical mechanics was mostly developed in these locations. Galileo's new theory of motion, for example, was highly dependent on what he learned at the Venetian arsenal, while his new astronomy

**26** Valleriani 2010; Bennett 2006.

**27** Feingold and Navarro-Brotons 2006.

**28** Boschiero 2007.

**29** Biagioli 1993; Valleriani 2010.

emerged at the Medici Court in Florence. This was the rule rather than the exception, and it applied to the system of religious education as well.

The broad framework of pre-classical mechanics was neither entirely coherent nor revolutionary in modern terms, but it was nonetheless capable of incorporating both ancient and modern elements. For example, Galileo's discourse on buoyancy and his law of free fall, and Kepler's *camera obscura*, were incorporated into the Catholic educational system.[30] Jesuits played a major role in inventing sophisticated mechanisms of inclusion and control that allowed for maintaining the Tridentine Aristotelian-Thomistic worldview while adapting innovations in order to present them as somehow related to the tradition. Many denounced the Jesuits for their techniques of fusing the new into the old in non-conventional ways. They were blamed for hypocrisy and accused of duplicity. Others preferred using the term *dissimulazione onesta* to describe the Jesuits' accommodation strategies. Yet the Jesuits well represented the option of taking part in modernity, and even shaping it, while still remaining faithful to tradition.

A concrete example will complete this short introduction to the problematics of Catholicism and modernity.

## Wonderful Machines in Jesuit Schools

The Jesuits were the most ambitious educational innovators in the Catholic world. Although their teaching was first justified in terms of the need to train confessors and preachers, the Society's rapid expansion necessitated a broader scope of activities. These were justified in practical terms, for the usefulness of the knowledge transmitted to students and the utility of this educational activity to the goals of society. Between the sixteenth and eighteenth centuries, for more than 200 years, most of the Catholic elite, and Catholic scientists in particular, were educated and socialized in Jesuit schools. The Jesuits cared for more than 200,000 children and adolescents each year, and they produced the likes of Torricelli, Descartes, Mersenne, Fontenelle, Laplace, Volta, Diderot, Helvétius, Condorcet, Turgot, Voltaire, Vico and Muratori, to name but a few of their most famous students.[31] Jesuit schools were the first in Europe in which mathematics was taught to all students of philosophy during the second year of studies. They thus took upon themselves the role of providing large audiences of students with

---

**30** Feldhay 2011.

**31** Gorman 2003:38.

some kind of scientific literacy, and small groups of students with a much more advanced level of physico-mathematical knowledge.

I wish to focus on a text entitled *Terra machinis mota*, written by the Jesuit mathematician Paolo Casati (1617–1707) and first published in 1655.[32] It is a fictional trialogue between Galileo Galilei (1564–1642); Marin Mersenne (1588–1648), a French Minim father and physico-mathematician; and Paulus Guldin (1577–1643), a Jesuit who authored three volumes on centers of gravity. The text, which includes five dissertations, discusses different kinds of mathematical solutions to the question of how much power would be required to move the globe of the earth out of its place by means of a mechanical device, demonstrating the Jesuits' success in accommodating Galileo's early mechanical project to the framework of their mathematical program of teaching.[33] Galileo's project is basically a fusion of elements borrowed from an ancient pseudo-Aristotelian text on mechanical questions with the mathematical approach of Archimedes and a new interpretation of these elements. Thus, it could fit the Jesuits' commitment to the Aristotelian scientific tradition and to their own participation in the Archimedean revival that had taken place some decades earlier. Casati's text manages to legitimize Galileo's general physico-mathematical approach while criticizing some of its premises (mainly Galileo's insistence on the possibility of a vacuum, which Casati rejected), and it also makes a case for diffusing the idea of a moving earth as a physical possibility, albeit not a Copernican one. Needless to say, all this took place some twenty-two years after Galileo's trial in 1633.

Now, a few words about the Jesuit author. Casati[34] was a well known figure in the seventeenth century, and not only for his series of physico-mathematical works, which were widely read. Of noble origin, and graced with the looks, manner and rhetorical talent of a typical Italian *gentiluomo*, he was chosen by his order's superiors for a delicate mission at the court of Queen Christina of Sweden, to which he set himself in 1652. Casati was expected to converse with the queen on Galileo's *Dialogue* and other scientific and philosophical issues, while helping her accomplish her wish to convert to Catholicism. This she finally did after abdicating from the Crown of Sweden, turning her back on her original Protestant religion and transferring her residence to Rome.

---

**32** Casati 1658.

**33** Feldhay 2006.

**34** For good account of Casati's life and work see Gavagna 1998:3–15; see also eadem 1995. Duhem dedicated a chapter to Jesuit treatises on statics in Duhem 1905, II: Chap. 16. For a recent account of Casati's visit to Queen Christina of Sweden see Gorman 1999:189.

Casati, who had started teaching mathematics at the Collegio Romano two years earlier, was well rewarded by his order. In 1657 he was moved to the Venice area, where he performed a series of prominent roles in the Jesuit administration, occasionally serving as professor of mathematics in Parma and confessor to two successive duchesses. At the same time he became one of the most authoritative writers in a tradition of "Jesuit mechanics." In 1684, he published his *Mechanicorum libri octo*,[35] the first attempt at a systematic synthesis of mechanics[36] before the publication of Newton's *Principia*. In the 1680s he was involved in a large-scale project, initiated in Ferrara and endorsed by the Pope, that attempted to canalize the Reno and Po rivers.[37] Casati's participation points to his practical scientist-engineer orientation.

The story of Casati's life well exemplifies the typical career trajectory of successful Jesuit physico-mathematicians–theologians. After completing a trilingual stage of humanistic studies and a three-year program in Aristotelian philosophy, they were entitled to one or two years of training in an advanced seminar called an "academy," where they acquainted themselves with the most updated scientific-engineering knowledge. The next stage of their education was a four-year course in theology, during which they also used to teach humanistic/rhetorical skills. From that point on, their expertise in mathematics was expressed mainly in teaching and writing. Many received the status of *scriptor* and dedicated themselves to writing in the later stages of their lives. In addition, they were often appointed by the Pope or other monarchs to carry out sensitive diplomatic missions, and they served as confessors and took part, as technical advisors, in mechanical projects.

Casati's five dissertations were rooted in a wider Jesuit discursive tradition. In a letter to the readers of his *Terra machinis mota*, Casati mentions a "mathematical problem" discussed at the the Collegio Romano, the prestigious Jesuit university in Rome, in the presence of the eminent prince Cardinal Langravius and of well known Roman *virtuosi*, as well as members of the high clergy and the nobility. In Jesuit scientific culture of those days, the public discussion of mathematical problems became a kind of ritual, a display of knowledge close in spirit to the *disputatio* and the public defense of theses.[38] Thus, the 1591 edition of the Jesuit *Ratio Studiorum* included a decision to "celebrate" publicly the solution of mathematical problems by students.

---

**35** Casati 1684.

**36** Baldini 1992:267, n. 52.

**37** Gavagna 1998:13–14.

**38** Gorman 2003:1–120.

## Conclusions

This paper suggests an outline for an archeology of the knowledge–religion–state configuration in Catholic Europe between around 1550 and 1650.

My conceptual and disciplinary point of departure is a reflection on the nature of prominent scientific and artistic discourses of the time, first and foremost the discourse on mechanics, which I, following others, have called "pre-classical mechanics." This body of knowledge – about to transform into Newtonian classical mechanics, the core discipline of modern physics – could be adapted perfectly to the utilitarian needs of the early modern sovereign state, which became engaged in supporting and promoting it in many ways.

Pre-classical mechanics combined ancient theoretical bodies of knowledge, such as the Aristotelian theory of motion and the Archimedean theory of buoyancy, with new, practical applications for solving problems, such as the trajectory of cannonballs or the motion of pendulums. For the first time, a systematic feedback loop between theory and practice eroded the rigid intellectual and social boundaries between physics, as part of the ancient philosophical Aristotelian corpus, and the mechanical arts, which had partly been theorized in antiquity but remained mainly in the domain of shipbuilders, the military, architects and constructors. In the process, the ancient, academic scientific–philosophical tradition conceived in terms of "theory," as well as its high-status carriers, opened up their boundaries toward new experiences accumulated in the fields of war or the production of machines for economic needs. Thus, while the preconditions for the emergence of the "new science" were created by the transformation of ancient bodies of knowledge, reflection and the erosion of intellectual and social boundaries, the new military and economic needs of rulers made scientific knowledge produced under the new conditions relevant and useful. Similarly, the new techniques of representation – in sculpture, painting or historical narratives – perfectly suited the needs of both sovereign rulers and science practitioners for legitimization.

In his book *The Portrait of the King*, Louis Marin[39] has analyzed the nature of representation as a mechanism of power duplication. Representation replaces real presence and creates the effect of presence even in the absence of the person represented, while also conferring validity and credibility upon them. Marin shows the power invested in representation and gained by rulers who patronized artists and scientists, but also the mutual dependency between rulers and the scientists and artists who enjoyed their patronage.

---

**39** Marin 1988.

The precariousness of the sovereign power of princes peeping through Bodin's text, and the scientists' efforts to transform theoretical-authoritative bodies of knowledge through practical applications and reflection on their effects, provide the background to understanding the mutual dependencies of political rulers and practitioners of science and the arts in sixteenth–seventeenth century Europe. Using the example of Casati, I have attempted to reconstruct how these interactions were mediated by new types of religious institutions. Casati's story, including his scientific training and the trajectory of his career, as well as the political context in Parma, where he operated, offer historical evidence for the kind of early modernity that developed in Catholicism in the sixteenth–seventeenth centuries.

The recitation of Casati's problem about a mechanical device capable of moving the globe expresses one facet of a religious culture rich in scientific, philosophical, historical, literary and theological contents and tightly connected to sovereign rulers. Parma, where Casati taught for thirty years, was then the capital of the rich and successful sovereign dukes of the Farnese family. In 1600, the Jesuits had been invited by the Duke to assist in building up a system of higher education in their state. Eventually, they controlled three prestigious interrelated institutions in the city: the old university, a Jesuit college and a *collegio dei nobili* that educated the sons of noble families from all over Europe.[40]

Under the rule of the Farnese, the Jesuits did not exclude fashionable activities such as theater and ballet from their schools. Descriptions of their venues for public intellectual activities exist and demonstrate a growing tendency toward refinement and grandeur. One example is a description, accompanied by a series of aquarelles, of the great hall at the Collegio dei Nobili, which displayed images of music, geography and dance derived from Greek and Roman mythology. Very often, such mythological representations told allegorical stories of contemporary rulers that propagated and legitimized their personal grandeur and that of their regimes.

The Jesuits started to build the foundations for mass secondary and higher education, which included professional training for scientist-engineers no less than for the clergy, bringing together general, humanistic education with moral formation.[41] Their culture was certainly modern in its general orientation to the active life of the present. But they were simultaneously traditional in their strong adherence to a holy message that could clearly be traced back, by authoritative

**40** Brizzi 1980; Baldini 2002; Turrini 2006.
**41** Feldhay 1995.

witnesses, to the historical beginning of Christianity. The Jesuits thus exemplified the kind of "traditional" modernity that I have tried to adumbrate in this paper.

## References

Baldini, Ugo. 1983. "Christoph Clavius and the Scientific Scene in Rome." In: G.V. Coyne, M.A. Hoskin and G. Pedersen (eds.), *Gregorian Reform of the Calendar: Proceedings of the Vatican Conference to Commemorate Its 400th Anniversary, 1582–1982*. Vatican: Pontifical Academy of Sciences – Vatican Observatory.

Baldini, Ugo. 1992. "Archimede nel seicento italiano." In: Corrado Dollo (ed.), *Archimede: Mito Tradizione Scienza*. Florence: Olschki.

Baldini, Ugo. 2002. "S. Rocco e la scuola scientifica della provincia veneta: Il quadro storico (1600–1773)." In: Roberto Greci and Gian Paolo Brizzi (eds.), *Gesuiti e università in Europa: Secoli 16–18 – Atti del Convegno di Studi Parma 13–15 dicembre 2001*. Bologna: Clueb. 283–323.

Bennett, Jim. 2006. "The Mechanical Arts." In: Katharine Park and Lorraine Daston (eds.), *The Cambridge History of Science: Early Modern Science*. Cambridge: Cambridge University Press. 677–695.

Biagioli, Mario. 1993. *Galileo, Courtier: The Practice of Science in the Culture of Absolutism*. Chicago: University of Chicago Press.

Blackwell, Richard. 1998. "Could There Be Another Galileo Case?" In: Peter Machamer (ed.), *The Cambridge Companion to Galileo*. Cambridge: Cambridge University Press.

Bodin, Jean.1967 [1576]. *Six Books of the Commonwealth* (English transl. by M.J. Tooley). Oxford: Blackwell.

Boschiero, Luciano. 2007. *Experiment and Natural Philosophy in Seventeenth-Century Tuscany: The History of the Accademia del Cimento*. Dordrecht: Springer.

Brizzi, Gian Paolo. 1980. "Educare il Principe, formare le élites: I gesuiti e Ranuccio I Farnese." In: idem et al. (eds.), *Università, Principe, Gesuiti: La politica farnesiana dell'istruzione a Parma e Piacenza (1545–1622)*. Rome: Bulzoni.

Casati, Paolo. 1684. *Mechanicorum libri octo*. Lyon: Ioan Posuel & Claudium Rigaud.

Casati, Paolo. 1658. *Terra machinis mota: Dissertationes geometricae, mechanicae, physicae, hydrostaticae*. Rome: De Lazaris.

Clavius, Christoph. 1603. *Romani Calendarii a Gregorio XIII. P.M: Restituti explicatio*. Rome: A. Zannettus.

Duhem, Pierre. 1905. *Les Origines de la Statique*. Paris: Librairie Scientifique A. Hermann.

Eisenstadt, Shmuel. 2000. "Multiple Modernities." *Daedalus*, 129:1–29.

Elshtain, Jean Bethke. 2008. *Sovereignty: God, State, and Self*. New York: Basic Books.

Feingold, Mordechai, and Victor Navarro-Brotons (eds.). 2006. *Universities and Science in the Early Modern Period*. Dordrecht: Springer.

Feldhay, Rivka. 1995. *Galileo and the Church: Political Inquisition or Critical Dialogue?* New York: Cambridge University Press.

Feldhay, Rivka. 2006. "On Wonderful Machines: The Transmission of Mechanical Knowledge by Jesuits." *Science and Education*, 15/2–4:151–172

Feldhay, Rivka. 2011. "The Jesuits: Transmitters of the New Science." In: Massimo Bucciantini, Michele Camerota and Franco Guidice (eds.), *Il Caso Galileo: Una rilettura storica, filosofica, teologica*. Florence: Olschki. 47–74.

Gavagna, Veronica. 1995. “L’Opera Scientifica di Paolo Casati (1617–1707).” Ph.D. Dissertation, University of Florence.

Gavagna, Veronica. 1998. “Il carteggio Casati (1642–1695),” *Bollettino di storia delle scienze matematiche*, 18:3–153.

Gorman, Michael John. 1999. “From ‘The Eyes of All’ to ‘Usefull Quarries in Philosophy and Good Literature’: Consuming Jesuit Science, 1600–1665.” In: J.W. O’Malley et al. (eds.), *The Jesuits: Cultures, Sciences, and the Arts, 1540–1773*. Toronto: University of Toronto Press.

Gorman, Michael John. 2003. “Mathematics and Modesty in the Society of Jesus: The Problems of Christoph Grienberger.” In: Mordechai Feingold (ed.), *The New Science and Jesuit Science: Seventeenth Century Perspectives* (Archimedes, 6). Dordrecht: Springer.

Grimm, Dieter. 2015. *Sovereignty: The Origin and Future of a Political and Legal Concept*. New York: Columbia University Press.

Hent, Kalmo, and Quentin Skinner (eds.). 2010. *Sovereignty in Fragments: The Past, Present and Future of a Contested Concept*. Cambridge: Cambridge University Press.

Heilbron, John L. (ed.). 2003. *The Oxford Companion to the History of Modern Science*. Oxford: Oxford University Press.

Hooykaas, Reijer. 1972. *Religion and the Rise of Modern Science*. Vancouver: Regent College Publishing.

Laird, Walter Roy, and Sophie Roux (eds.). 2008. *Mechanics and Natural Philosophy before the Scientific Revolution*. Dordrecht: Springer.

Marin, Louis. 1988 [1981]. *Portrait of the King* (English transl. by Martha M. Houle). Dordrecht: Springer.

Meli, Domenico Bertoloni. 2006. *Thinking with Objects: The Transformation of Mechanics in the Seventeenth Century*. Baltimore: Johns Hopkins University Press.

Merton, Robert K. 1970. *Science, Technology, and Society in Seventeenth-Century England*. New York: H. Fertig. (First published in *Osiris*, 4 [1938]:360–632.)

North, J.D. 1983. “The Western Calendar – ‘Intolerabilis, Horribilis, et Derisibilis’: Four Centuries of Discontent.” In: G.V. Coyne, M.A. Hoskin and G. Pedersen (eds.), *Gregorian Reform of the Calendar: Proceedings of the Vatican Conference to Commemorate Its 400th Anniversary, 1582–1982*. Vatican: Pontifical Academy of Sciences – Vatican Observatory.

Ophir, Adi. 2010. “State.” *Mafte’akh: Lexical Review of Political Thought*, 1e:67–96. At: http://mafteakh.tau.ac.il/en/2010-01/05/.

Prodi, Paolo. 1982. *The Papal Prince – One Body and Two Souls: The Papal Monarchy in Early Modern Europe* (English transl. by S. Haskins). Cambridge: Cambridge University Press.

Prodi, Paolo. 2000. *Una storia della giustizia: Dal pluralismo dei fori ad moderno dualismo fra coscienza e dirrito*. Bologna: Il Mollino.

Reinhard, Wolfgang. 1977. “Gegenreformation als Modernisierung? Prolegomena zu einer Theorie des konfessionellen Zeitalters.” *Archiv für Reformationsgeschichte*, 68:226–229.

Reinhard, Wolfgang. 1989. “Reformation, Counter-Reformation, and the Early Modern State: A Reassessment.” *Catholic Historical Review*, 75/3:383–404.

Renn, Jürgen, and Peter McLaughlin. 2018. “The Balance, the Lever, and the Aristotelian Origins of Mechanics.” In: Rivka Feldhay, Jürgen Renn, Matthias Schemmel and Matteo Valleriani (eds.), *Emergence and Expansion of Pre-Classical Mechanics* (Boston Studies in the Philosophy of Science, 271). Dordrecht: Springer.

Shea, William R. 1986. “Galileo and the Church.” In: David C. Lindberg and Ronald L. Numbers (eds.), *God & Nature: Historical Essays on the Encounter between Christianity and Science*. Berkeley: University of California Press.

Smith, Wilfred Cantwell. 1979. *Faith and Belief*. Princeton: Princeton University Press.
Smith, Wilfred Cantwell. 1991 [1963]. *The Meaning and End of Religion: A New Approach to the Religious Traditions of Mankind*. Minneapolis: Fortress Press.
Turrini, Miriam. 2006. *Il "giovin signore" in collegio: I gesuiti e l'educazione della nobiltà nelle consuetudini del collegio ducale di Parma*. Bologna: Clueb.
Valleriani, Matteo. 2010. "Was Galileo an Engineer?" In: Idem, *Galileo Engineer*. Dordrecht: Springer. 193–211.
Ziggelaar, A. 1983. "The Papal Bull of 1582 Promulgating a Reform of the Calendar." In: G.V. Coyne, M.A. Hoskin and G. Pedersen (eds.), *Gregorian Reform of the Calendar: Proceedings of the Vatican Conference to Commemorate Its 400th Anniversary, 1582–1982*. Vatican: Pontifical Academy of Sciences – Vatican Observatory.

Paul Mendes-Flohr

# Jewish Intellectuals on the Chimera of Progress: Walter Benjamin, Martin Buber and Leo Strauss

The Jewish experience of modernity is haunted by an intractable paradox. On the one hand, the Jews are arguably the preeminent representatives of the modern cultural ethos. As Yuri Slezkine provocatively argues in *The Jewish Century*:

> The Modern Age is the Jewish Age. ... Modernization is about everyone becoming urban, mobile, literate, articulate, intellectually intricate, physically fastidious, and occupationally flexible. It is about learning how to cultivate people and symbols, not fields and herds. It is about pursuing wealth for the sake of learning, learning for the sake of wealth, and both wealth and learning for their own sake. It is about transforming peasants and princes into merchants and priests, replacing inherited privilege with acquired prestige, and dismantling social estates for the benefit of individuals, nuclear families, and book-reading tribes (nations). Modernization, in other words, is about everyone becoming Jews.[1]

To strengthen the rhetorical effect of this deliberately hyperbolic observation, Slezkine adds: "No one is better at being Jewish" – that is, modern – "than Jews themselves."[2]

But the Jews' entry into the modern world may also be viewed as emblematic of the agonies of modernity. Although the Jews adapted with exemplary versatility and seeming ease to modern economy and culture, it has also been observed that they "did not enter the modern European society in a long process of 'endogenous' gestation and growth, but they plunged into it as the ghetto walls were being breached, with a bang, though not without prolonged whimpers."[3] Hence, the Jews were not only beneficiaries of modernity but also its victims. The role many Jews played as some of the most energetic and creative agents of modernity only serves to becloud the spiritual – not to speak of the physical – wounds that

**1** Slezkine 2004:1.

**2** *Ibid.* Slezkine also underscores that "the Jews did not launch the Modern Age. They joined it late, had little to do with some of its most important episodes (such as the Scientific and Industrial Revolutions), and labored arduously to adjust to its many demands. They just did better than most – and reshaped the modern world as a consequence – but they were not present at the creation and missed out on some of the early role assignments." *Ibid.*:64.

**3** Werblowsky 1976:42.

https://doi.org/10.1515/9783110723984-005

their passage into a modern, secular order entailed. Due to the peculiar dialectics of Jewish emancipation, those wounds were not easily cauterized, and they continue to fester.

The votaries of the Jews' liberation from the ghettos – and integration into the social and economic fabric of Europe – demanded that they free themselves of the shackles of their anachronistic "oriental" religion and "backward" customs. The eminent advocate of Enlightenment and tolerance, Immanuel Kant, called upon the Jews to "throw off the garb of [their] ancient cult, which now serves no purpose and even suppresses any true religious attitude."[4] The "euthanasia of Judaism," as Kant unabashedly described this process, would enhance the prospects of the Jews' emancipation, for it would "quickly call attention to them as an educated and civilized people who are ready for all the rights of citizenship."[5] "Educated and civilized" are, of course, loaded terms that bear a bivalent message. On the hand, they signal that the Jews are perceived as not "educated" or "civilized," according to the standards of "enlightened" Europe. On the other hand, they intimate that the Jews' emancipation is subject to their adoption of the standards of education and culture of enlightened, bourgeois Europe.

Indeed, this is how the Jews understood the challenge posed to them by the Enlightenment's vision of their emancipation. Accordingly, they established societies to further Jewish integration through self-reformation. In December 1819, at the founding meeting in Berlin of one such society, the Verein für Wissenschaft der Juden, Leopold Zunz, a 25-year-old university student who would go on to become a pioneer of modern Jewish studies, delivered a lecture on "Judenübel" (Jewish evils), faults that required immediate remedy. His list of several dozen putative failings in need of prompt attention included the spirit of petty trade, contempt of science, outdated, destructive and meaningless customs, lack of appreciation of secular knowledge and "coarseness in their speech, comportment, and manners."[6] Zunz's delineation of the "evils" of his fellow Jews manifestly echoes Kant's complaint – frequently iterated in various formulations by both votaries and opponents of the Enlightenment and the nascent liberal political order. Jews quickly got the message: They would seek to become "educated and civilized," and they did so with extraordinary alacrity – with a wary eye on their brethren who were slow to follow their example.

The price of internalizing the prevailing negative images of Jews and Judaism was a loss of self-esteem, which ever-increasingly led to the conclusion that one's

4 Kant 1996:274.
5 *Ibid.*:275.
6 Zunz 2011 (1819).

ancestral religion and culture were an impediment to acceptance by the hegemonic social and cultural order. In this respect, the acculturation and subsequent assimilation of European Jewry were akin to what the Caribbean philosopher Franz Fanon analyzed as the psychological effects of colonization: the wearing of "white masks," as he poetically put it, to camouflage "black faces." Under the imperious tutelage of colonization, acculturation amounted to an existentially false and degrading existence. "The colonized is elevated above his jungle status in proportion to his adoption of the mother country's cultural standards. He becomes whiter as he renounces his blackness, his jungle."[7] To be sure, there are far-reaching social and political differences between the colonization of indigenous populations and the emancipation of European Jewry. But existentially there are profound similarities. The assimilation of the Jews – like that of the colonized blacks of France's Caribbean colonies – was not merely a process of secularization or, if you will, modernization. It was often accompanied by, as Fanon put it with respect to colonized blacks, "the internalization – or, better, the epidermalization – of [their alleged] inferiority."[8] With respect to Jews, this process led in the extreme to Jewish self-hatred, and more frequently to a contemptuous embarrassment about their "uncivilized" co-religionists.

Although the assimilation of European Jewry bears many of the degrading marks of colonization, its dynamic ultimately was different. Given the Enlightenment's valorization of reason and vision of a Republic of Letters open in principle to all human beings, Jews adopted the pursuit of education as their overarching strategy to gain acceptance. More precisely, they embraced the ideal of *Bildung*, which conflated European literary culture with bourgeois aesthetic and social values. To be sure, the rush to join the *Bildungsbourgeoisie* was more often than not rebuffed,[9] yielding, as Hannah Arendt ironically observed, not the hoped-for acceptance but merely a "well-furnished library."[10] That library

---

**7** Fanon 1967 (1952):18. Cf. *ibid.*:122: "At first thought it might seem strange that the anti-Semite's outlook should be related to that of the Negrophobe. It was my philosophy professor, a native of the Antilles, who recalled the fact to me one day: 'Whenever you hear anyone abuse the Jews, pay attention, because he is talking about you.' And I found that he was universally right – by which I meant that I was answerable in my body and in my heart for what was done to my brother. Later I realized that he meant, quite simply, an anti-Semite is inevitably anti-Negro."

**8** *Ibid.*:13.

**9** Cf. Hundt-Radowsky 2011 (1819): "I do not deny in the least that Jews are able to acquire scholarly knowledge. But such knowledge never ennobles their spirit or feelings. ... I claim that the Jew is incapable of becoming a scholar: that is a man who benefits the world through his spirit and learning and is instrumental in the further education of his contemporaries for posterity."

**10** Arendt-Stern 2013 (1933):17.

was dominated, of course, by the classics of German and world literature and *ipso facto* displaced the writings of traditional Jewish learning. But the acculturation of European Jewry not only entailed deracination and a severance from the intellectual and spiritual world of Judaism; for many, it also engendered no small measure of embarrassment about their origins, along with what Kafka so poignantly described as the tragic antinomy of modern Jewish existence. Most Jews, he observed, would have liked "to leave Jewishness behind them," but they were not able fully to do so. Hence, "with their hind legs they were still glued to their father's Jewishness and with their waving front legs they found no new ground."[11] "The Jew," wrote Martin Buber, "is not the same person he once was; he has passed through every heaven and hell of the Occident, and his soul has come to grief."[12]

Walter Benjamin, "the taxonomist of sadness,"[13] spoke of the desiccation of the Jew's ancestral patrimony as a "decay of aura" inducing an insidious melancholy,[14] which, Gillian Rose suggests, is captured by the rabbinic concept of the *agunah*, "the deserted wife, who has not been sent a bill of divorce and does not know if her husband is still alive."[15] Without the so-called *get* in hand, the *agunah* may not remarry, "nor does she know whether she may embark on mourning."[16] Kafka's Jew, too, is akin to the *agunah*, paralyzed by a catatonic sense of bereavement and thus unable – perhaps simply not prepared – to mourn and work through his loss. Walter Benjamin attributed Kafka's malady (and apparently his own) to the loss of a tradition that can be neither retrieved nor adequately replaced. In a letter to Gershom Scholem, penned in June 1938, he discussed at length Kafka's work, which, as he put it, "represents tradition falling ill." Tellingly, he elaborates his diagnosis by drawing upon the talmudic distinction between *halakhah*, the substance of Jewish tradition as articulated in rules and rituals, and *aggadah*, the narrative commentary:

---

**11** Kafka 1977:288f.
**12** Buber 1967:77.
**13** Rose 1998:88.
**14** *Ibid.* For a detailed analysis of Benjamin's concept of melancholy, see Ferber 2013.
**15** Cf. Rose 1998:88–89: "The object, style and mood of Benjamin's philosophy converge, not in the Christian mournfulness or melancholy, discerned from the Baroque *Trauerspiel* to Baudelaire, but in the Judaic state of desertion – in Hebrew, *agunah* – the stasis which his agon with the law dictates. ... [T]he dialectical image of the baroque melancholy is the *agunah* – the deserted wife. ... In the tales of the modern Hebrew writer S.J. Agnon, which Benjamin cherished, everybody is in a state of desertion, including the *Shekinah*, the Divine Presence in the world."
**16** *Ibid.*:89.

> Wisdom has sometimes been defined as the epic side of truth. Such a definition marks wisdom off as a property of tradition; it is truth in its aggadic consistency (*hagadischen Konsistenz*).[17] It is this consistency of truth (*diese Konsistenz der Wahrheit*) that has been lost.[18]

Benjamin goes on to observe that in this respect Kafka was not unique, for he "was far from being the first to face this situation. Many had accommodated themselves to it, clinging to the truth [of tradition] or whatever they regarded as such, and with a more or less heavy heart, had renounced [its] transmissibility."[19] But Kafka's struggle with tradition was different. "Kafka's real genius," Benjamin explains to Scholem, "was that he tried something entirely new: He sacrificed truth for the sake of clinging to transmissibility, to its [the tradition's] aggadic element." To be sure, Kafka's *aggadah* is a narrative commentary on a tradition and its wisdom that are lost; hence, his is an equivocal narrative, for it relates simply the sense of loss; indeed, it is uncertain what precisely is lost. In this respect, Kafka's writings are "by their very nature parables." But, Benjamin adds, "that is their misery and their beauty, that they had to become *more* than parables. They do not modestly lie at the feet of doctrine, as *aggadah* lies at the feet of *halakhah*."[20] When Kafka's parables "have crouched down, they unexpectedly raise a mighty paw" against doctrine, against tradition. And "this is why, in the case of Kafka, we can no longer speak of wisdom. Only the products of its decay remain."[21]

Although Kafka's plight may be specifically Jewish, Benjamin regards it as a barometer of the ominous course that modernity has taken. With uncanny prescience, he comments in his letter to Scholem, posted five months before *Kristallnacht* and fourteen months before the German invasion of Poland and the beginning of World War II, that:

> The long and short of it is that clearly an appeal had to be made to nothing less than the forces of this tradition if an individual (by the name of Franz Kafka) was to be confronted with *that* reality of ours which is projected theoretically, for example, in modern physics, and practically in the technology of warfare. What I meant to say is that this reality can scarcely still be experienced by an *individual*, and that Kafka's world … is the exact complement of his epoch, an epoch that is preparing itself to annihilate the inhabitants of this planet on a massive scale. This experience that

**17** Benjamin and Scholem 1989:272.
**18** Benjamin to Scholem, June 12, 1938, in Benjamin and Scholem 1992:225.
**19** *Ibid.*
**20** *Ibid.*
**21** *Ibid.*

> corresponds to that of Kafka as a private individual will probably first become accessible to the masses at such time as they are about to be annihilated.[22]

For Benjamin, Kafka thus was emblematic of the failure of modernity, or more precisely, of the myth of progress. On the eve of his desperate and ultimately fruitless attempt to flee the fate that awaited European Jewry, he formulated his last work, "On the Concept of History," better known as "Theses on the Philosophy of History." In the ninth thesis, Angelus Novus, with a frightened, nay, catatonic gaze looks back at the trajectory of history and declares it "one single catastrophe." And yet he concludes his ruminations by retrieving hope from the rubble of history and the delusory myth of progress:

> We know that the Jews were prohibited from investigating the future. The Torah and the prayers instruct them in remembrance, however. This stripped the future of its magic, to which all those succumb who turn to the soothsayers for enlightenment. This does not imply, however, that for the Jews the future turned into homogeneous, empty time. For every second of time was the strait gate through which Messiah might enter.[23]

But this affirmation of hope is not devoid of a touch of irony, if read in light of what, in another letter to Scholem, he refers to as "the Kafkaesque formulation of the categorical imperative: 'Act in such a way that the angels have something to do.'"[24] The angels bear, however, as Kafka also notes, "an abundance of hope, but not for us."[25] Moreover, should "the Messiah come," he will arrive "when he is no longer needed."[26]

In his rejection of the certitudes and pieties of the modern ethos, Benjamin is widely regarded – indeed, celebrated – as the quintessential German-Jewish intellectual. The sociologist Zgymunt Bauman attributes Benjamin's critical posture to an existential condition "shared with most intellectuals – that of exile."[27] As a mode of being, the "purpose [of exile] is to be elsewhere."[28] But the longing to be elsewhere "consists in the incessant labor" of endeavoring to bring exile to an end, while at the same time deeming the belief that the end is nigh "is a disaster" comparable to "abandoning efforts to make that belief true."[29] As a paradox-

**22** *Ibid.*:224.
**23** Benjamin 1964:264.
**24** Benjamin to Scholem, April 14, 1938, in Benjamin and Scholem 1992:216.
**25** Cited by Benjamin in his letter to Scholem, June 12, 1938, *ibid.*:225.
**26** Kafka 1991:28.
**27** Bauman 1998:72.
**28** *Ibid.*
**29** *Ibid.*:73.

ical cognitive sensibility, exile engenders a resistance to all absolute and fixed intellectual positions.

Thorstein Veblen construed such an intellectual orientation as "the skeptical frame of mind" he deemed necessary for scientific and scholarly innovation. It was precisely this skeptical disposition, he held, that explained "the intellectual preeminence of European Jews."[30] The state of mind that Bauman describes as an exilic longing to be elsewhere, Veblen attributes to the social and cultural marginality of Jews who entered the modern world. Finding themselves in a liminal space between their ancestral community and that of the non-Jewish world , they were free of "the inhibitions of intellectual quietism" that bind one to convention and given beliefs:

> The intellectually gifted Jew is in a peculiarly fortunate position in respect of this requisite immunity from the inhibitions of intellectual quietism. But he can come in for such immunity only at the cost of losing his secure place in the scheme of conventions into which he has been born, and at the cost, also, of finding no similarly secure place in that scheme of gentile conventions into which he is thrown. For him as for other men in the like case, the skepticism that goes to make him an effectual factor in the increase and diffusion of knowledge among men involves a loss of that peace of mind that is the birthright of the safe and sane quietist. He becomes a disturber of the intellectual peace, but only at the cost of becoming an intellectual wayfaring man, a wanderer in the intellectual no-man's-land, seeking another place to rest, farther along the road, somewhere over the horizon.[31]-

Veblen thus ascribed the creativity of the Jewish intellectuals to their social marginality. This thesis may be further nuanced by reference to Georg Simmel's essay on "The Stranger" (*Der Fremde*). Unlike the tourist or refugee, "who comes today and goes tomorrow," observed Simmel, the stranger is or rather has become a member of the society in which s/he dwells: She or he is a person "who comes today and stays tomorrow."[32] The stranger's position in the group in which he is now a member "is fundamentally affected by the fact that he does not belong in it initially and that he brings qualities into it that are not, and cannot, be indigenous to it."[33]As a result, the stranger, as Simmel paradoxically puts it, is "near and far at the same time."[34] Like Veblen's marginal Jew, the stranger is "is freer ... practically and theoretically [than the native members of the group]; he examines conditions with less prejudice; he assesses them against standards

**30** Veblen 1998 (1919):219–231.
**31** *Ibid.*:227.
**32** Simmel 1971:143.
**33** *Ibid.*
**34** *Ibid.*:148.

that are more general and more objective; and his actions are not confined by custom, piety, and precedent."[35] The European Jew, whom Simmel seems to have had in mind, was such a stranger. By dint of his acculturation, he had become a cognitive insider, at home in the symbolic and intellectual discourse of his adopted culture. Yet, at the same, he remained by and large a social outsider. He was, in Simmel's terms, "near and far," a cognitive insider whose position as a social outsider encouraged the assumption of a critical perspective on the norms and values of the society to which he was now culturally and intellectually bound.

Hence, integrated in the cognitive universe of a given society, the stranger – here the European Jewish intellectual – focused his or her critical dissent on either the proximate or the ultimate norms and values of that society. The proximate norms and values are the operative practices that are meant to support the ultimate axio-normative principles of a society. In the name of personal freedom as a society's ultimate norm and ideal value, one may protest that certain prevailing or "proximate" practices actually undermine the realization of that norm and its attendant values. However, one may also find the ultimate axio-normative principles governing one's society to be fundamentally mistaken. In either case, the intellectual would voice axio-normative dissent within the cognitive universe of his or her society.

According to the degree and nature of their axio-normative dissent, European Jewish intellectuals may be cast as representing three typologically distinct postures: those who question the ultimate values and norms of society; those who critique its proximate values and norms from a conservative point of view; and those who do so from a liberal point of view. This typology of axio-normative dissent may be illustrated with respect to *a*, if not *the* key principle of Western modernity: The idea of progress as sponsored by the liberal ethos promoted by the Enlightenment. The first posture of this tripartite typology is one that questions the validity of the very idea of progress. This radical critique of the ultimate values and norms of society is represented by Walter Benjamin, whose Angel of History vehemently rejects the idea of progress. The second, conservative position is represented by Leo Strauss's advocacy of a retrieval of the medieval tension between Athens and Jerusalem – between Reason and Revelation – as a corrective to what he saw as the naïve, nihilistic conception of progress, which denies any source of meaning outside of history. The third position, the radical liberal critique of modernity, is represented by Martin Buber. Sharing Benjamin's and Strauss's anxiety about the destructive wiles of instrumental reason in politics and interpersonal relations, Buber enjoined a religious, dialogical humanism

35 *Ibid.*:146.

in order to secure the idea of progress and the vision of enhanced human dignity and fraternity between peoples.

While Benjamin, Strauss and Buber represent three distinct typological vectors of Jewish confrontations with modernity, each found themselves in the grips of what Strauss called a theological-political predicament. Each, from his distinctive perspective, diagnosed the ills of modernity as ensuing from the separation of theology from politics, or rather from the detachment of the quotidian concerns of politics and social life from the transcendent. For Benjamin, the wedding of the idea of progress with the natural sciences and the advances in technological and organizational calculations led to the imperious domination of instrumental reason over critical reason and the betrayal of the hopes humanity had placed in history under the aegis of the Enlightenment. This is the process Benjamin's colleagues Max Horkheimer and Theodor Adorno elaborated four years after his tragic death in their monumental study on the *Dialectic of Enlightenment* (1944).[36] Already in 1920 or 1921, in his "Theological-Political Fragment," Benjamin had exclaimed:

> Only the Messiah himself consummates all history, in the sense that he alone redeems, completes, creates its relation to the Messianic. For this reason nothing historical can relate itself on its own account to anything Messianic. Therefore the Kingdom of God is not the *telos* of the historical dynamic; it cannot be set as a goal [of history]. From the standpoint of history it [the Kingdom of God] is not the goal, but the end [*Ende*]. Therefore the order of the profane cannot be built up on the idea of the Divine Kingdom.[37]

This is not a testament of faith; for Benjamin was not a believer. It is rather the negative theology of a secular individual who has lost his faith in history. Indeed, for Benjamin history has no intrinsic *telos*. There is, as he learned from his friend and principal interlocutor on matters of religion and Judaism, Gershom Scholem, a radical disjunction between history and redemption. Although "every second of time [is] the strait gate in time through which the Messiah might enter," Benjamin placed hope, slight as it was, in a revolutionary resistance to history, in an effort to disrupt the ruthless flow of its evil logic. In the notes he jotted down in preparing his "Theses on the Philosophy of History," he muses: "Marx says that revolutions are the locomotive of world history. But perhaps it is quire otherwise. Perhaps revolutions are an attempt by the passengers of this train – namely, humanity – to activate the emergency brake."[38]

**36** Horkheimer and Adorno 1972.
**37** Benjamin 1978 (1920/1921?).
**38** Cited in Löwy 2005:66f.

Strauss shared Benjamin's anxiety about what they perceived to be liberalism's inability to direct the course of history and to confront the threat of fascism and totalitarian tyranny. He detected at the core of liberalism an underlying antinomy that, in his view, explains its political weakness. The conception of science as an objective, value-free discipline perforce induces a moral relativism that undermines liberalism's ability to justify its normative commitment to liberal ideals. The structural inability of liberal political culture to meet the challenges of moral and *a fortiori* political relativism was the overarching concern of Strauss's ramified writings in political philosophy. Restrained, indeed crippled by its value-neutrality, the modern liberal state is hard-pressed to justify its foundational values. Strauss located the roots of this paralyzing dilemma in the modern conception of natural rights, which he traced back to Hobbes. It was Hobbes, he declared, who sowed the seeds of the view that "all human thoughts or beliefs are historical,"[39] thus in effect denying the possibility of attaining any objective, trans-historical criteria by which to judge moral and political actions. Accordingly, Strauss revisited pre-modern political thought to probe the possibility of devising a concept of nature that would allow for some notion of absolute moral standards. In this context, he questioned the modern critique of religion, which had led to the dismissal of divine revelation as an epistemologically vacuous concept. Referring to a belief in revelation as orthodoxy, Strauss argued:

> The genuine refutation of orthodoxy would require the proof that the world and human life are perfectly intelligible without the assumption of a mysterious God; it would require at least the success of the philosophical system: man has to show himself theoretically and practically as the master of the world and the master of his life; the merely given must be replaced by the world created by man theoretically and practically.[40]

Like Benjamin's thinking on this score, Strauss's affirmation of the plausibility of revelation is not an expression of personal belief but rather an apophatic check on the hubris of modern rationalism and its claim to scientific omniscience. The subjection of all knowledge, including axio-normative judgments, to the epistemological scrutiny of science, Strauss averred, is "the root of all modern darkness from the seventeenth century on."[41] The modern valorization of reason as the sole arbiter of truth sets in motion a dialectic that initially obscures "the difference between theory and praxis, an obscuring that first leads to a reduction of praxis to theory (this is the meaning of so-called [modern] rationalism) and then,

**39** Strauss 1953:25.
**40** Strauss 1965:29
**41** Strauss 1993:66

in retaliation, to the rejection of theory in the name of praxis that is no longer intelligible as praxis."[42] This dialectic reaches its final and deleterious conclusion with Heidegger's radical historicism, which denies any meaning to reason outside of history. Thus, like Benjamin, Strauss gropes for a meta-historical principle, but not to overcome modernity. Rather, he sought to strengthen the liberal order by retrieving values and cognitive perspectives from pre-modern religious and philosophical culture.

Buber was also wary of the apotheosis of history represented by the idea of progress. He thus protested the ontological affirmation of history, inaugurated by Hegel and given frightful expression by Heidegger in his infamous rector's address of 1933:

> [As] for Hegel world history is the absolute process in which the spirit attains the consciousness of itself; so for Heidegger historical existence is the illumination of being; in neither is there room for a supra-historical reality that sees history and judges it.[43]

Appealing to the divine seat of judgment, Buber rejects the ontological presupposition of the Idea of Progress, the notion that "Die Weltgeschichte ist das Weltgericht" (the history of the world is the Last Judgment). Although history cannot take the place of God, it nonetheless is meaningful for Buber if man regards himself as "God's partner in the *dialogue* of history. The future is not fixed, for God wants man to come to Him with full freedom, to return to Him even out of a plight of extreme hopelessness."[44]

It is by virtue of the dialogue of history – in contrast to the dialectic of history – that man both establishes a relationship with God and is an agent of redemption; indeed, history will be pushed forward only if man remains in history. To heed the counsel of despair and withdraw from public life is to surrender history to the cynical forces that claim to control human destiny. Nor is one to secure the purity of one's soul and moral ideals by studied detachment from a corrupt world; such a posture amounts, as even Hegel noted, to a "self-willed impotence" (*eigensinnige Kraftlosigkeit*).[45] Personal and collective redemption, Buber insisted, is attained "not above the fray, but in it":[46] "The Word [of God] is not victorious in its purity, but in its corruption – it bears fruit in the *corruptio seminis*."[47]

---

**42** *Ibid.*
**43** Buber 1957c:215.
**44** Buber 1957b:198.
**45** Hegel 2010:487.
**46** Buber 1957a:137
**47** *Ibid.*:128.

Shortly after Hitler seized power, Buber addressed this message to German Jewry. Urging his beleaguered brethren to bear witness to the humanistic teachings of the Hebrew Scripture, he declared:

> Biblical humanism cannot, as does its Western counterpart, raise the individual above the problems of the moment; it seeks instead to train the person to stand fast in them, to prove himself in them. This stormy night, these shafts of lightning flashing down, this threat of destruction – Do not escape from them into a world of *logos*, of perfected form! Stand fast, hear the word in the thunder, obey, respond! This terrifying world is the world of God. It lays claim upon you. Prove yourself in it as a man of God![48]

It is significant – particularly in the context of the rise of the Third Reich – that Buber associates biblical humanism with "its Western counterpart." Although he was particularly attentive to the woes of his people – indeed, he was a Zionist – he understood the alleviation of their plight as intimately bound to rescuing the modern project, with its universal promise of *liberté, égalité, fraternité*. These triadic principles were central to the modern project as Buber understood it, and the common task of biblical and Western humanism was thus to ensure that they would prevail. European civilization faltered because it failed to appreciate that these principles are inherently bound to one another and can only flourish together as a unit. Buber expressed this vision, which he associated with the task of humanism, in the form of a midrashic parable:

> Three sisters were born into what was to be a happy family, but catastrophe struck them and they were separated, and torn from one another: One sister, *Égalité* by name, was taken to the East (where she was embraced by the Soviet bear), and one, *Liberté*, remained forlorn in the West (where she is hosted by liberal, capitalist democracies); the third sister, *Fraternité*, went astray and disappeared; no one knew where she had gone or whether she would ever return. In the meantime, the first two sisters – *Liberté* and *Égalité* – became estranged from one another and would often quarrel. Only when they were reunited would *Fraternité* reappear and join them, restoring the harmonious union of the sisters.[49]

It is the mandate of biblical and Western humanism, which Buber inflected with Utopian socialist values, to reunite the three sisters and thereby ensure that the project of modernity resumes its course toward, if not the Promised Land, then at least a more dignified future for *all* of humankind.

Despite the messianic tone of this vision, Buber was no Romantic. He soberly acknowledged that there could be no retreat from modernity to pre-modern

---

**48** Buber 2002 (1933):50.

**49** Buber 1952, an address given by Buber in West Germany in the framework of its first "Brotherhood Week," instituted in March 1952. My translation – P. M.-F.

civilization, nor a leap over it into the lap of the *eschaton*.[50] While still a young man, he initiated and edited a series of some forty monographs that, under the general title *Die Gesellschaft*, unambiguously affirmed modern, urban civilization. As defined by the 28-year-old Buber, the overarching question of these monographs – each dealing with a topic characteristic of urban modernity, such as "the department store," "strikes," "parliamentary politics," "the stock exchange," "journalism" and "the women's movement" – was the inter-human (*das Zwischenmenschliche*), the dynamic of intersubjective relations under the conditions of post-traditional social life.[51] This set the agenda of Buber's lifelong work. He drew inspiration, to be sure, from traditional Jewish sources, preeminently the Hebrew Bible and Hasidism, the east European movement of popular mysticism – but also from the writings of other faith communities, particularly Buddhism and Daoism.[52] His principal focus, however, was emphatically on the modern project, which he felt was plagued by internal contradictions. In his ramified writings, he identified the quintessential contradiction and thus the challenge posed by modernity as that between the compelling value placed on individualism – which by its very nature begets a competitive culture of meritocracy and personal mobility – and the ethical imperative to maintain community, attentive and compassionate interpersonal relations, and transcendent, universal values. As a Jew, he was committed to securing the cultural, communal and political dignity of his people, but he insisted that this objective must be attained without violating the humanistic ethos he deemed necessary to sustain the modern project.

In this respect, Buber shared with Walter Benjamin and Leo Strauss the theological-political predicament of modernity. In calling attention to this predicament, they also shared what the American sociologist Daniel Bell has described as "the plight – and glory – of the alienated Jewish intellectual," whose "role is to point to the need of brotherhood," though he is unable to "accept any embodiment of community as final. He can only live in permanent tension and as a permanent critic."[53]

---

**50** Cf. Buber 1957a:137: "We cannot prepare the messianic world, we can only prepare for it. There is no legitimately messianic, no legitimately messianic-intended politics."

**51** See Mendes-Flohr 1989:83–92, 127–130; and Wiehn 1992.

**52** See Buber 2014.

**53** Bell 2011 (1946):853.

## References

Arendt-Stern, Hannah. 2013 (1933). "Rahel Varnhagen and Goethe" (English transl. from the French by Haun Saussy). *Critical Inquiry*, 40/1:15–24.

Bauman, Zygmunt. 1998. "Walter Benjamin, the Intellectual." In: Marcus and Nead 1998.

Bell, Daniel. 2011 (1946). "A Parable of Alienation" (*Jewish Frontier*, November 1946). In: Mendes-Flohr and Reinharz 2011.

Benjamin, Walter. 1964. "Theses on the Philosophy of History." In: idem, *Illuminations*, ed. Hannah Arendt (English. transl. by Harry Zohn). New York: Schocken.

Benjamin, Walter. 1978 (1920/1921?). "Theologico-Political Fragment." In: idem, *Reflections: Essays, Aphorisms, Autobiographical Writings* (English transl. by Edmund Jephcott), ed. Peter Demetz. New York: Harcourt, Brace, Jovanovich. 312–313.

Benjamin, Walter, and Gershom Scholem. 1989. *Briefwechsel, 1933–1940*, ed. G. Scholem. Frankfurt a.M.: Suhrkamp.

Benjamin, Walter, and Gershom Scholem. *The Correspondence of Walter Benjamin and Gershom Scholem, 1932–1940* (English transl. by Gary Smith and Andre Lefevere), ed. Gershom Scholem. Cambridge, MA: Harvard University Press.

Buber, Martin. 1952. Ansprache zur Woche der Brüderlichkeit, 7.3.1952. National Library of Israel, Martin Buber Archive, Mappe 173.

Buber, Martin. 1957. *Pointing the Way: Collected Essays*, ed. and English transl. by Maurice Friedman. New York: Harper & Row.

Buber, Martin. 1957a. "Gandhi, Politics, and Us." In: Buber 1957.

Buber, Martin. 1957b. "Prophecy, Apocalyptic, and the Historical Hour." In: Buber 1957.

Buber, Martin. 1957c. "The Validity and Limitation of the Political Principle." In: Buber 1957.

Buber, Martin. 1967. "The Spirit of the Orient and Judaism" (English transl. by Eva Jospe). In: idem, *On Judaism*, ed. N.N. Glatzer. New York: Schocken.

Buber, Martin. 2002 (1933). "Biblical Humanism" (English translation of "Biblischer Humanismus," *Der Morgen*, 9/4). In: idem, *The Martin Buber Reader: Essential Writings*, ed. Asher D. Biemann. New York: Palgrave Macmillan.

Buber, Martin. 2014. *Schriften zur chinesischen Philosophie und Literatur* (Martin Buber Werkasugabe, 2.3), ed. Irene Eber. Gütersloh: Gütersloher Verlagshaus.

Fanon, Franz. 1967 (1952). *Black Skin, White Masks* (*Peau noire, masques blancs*; English transl. by Charles Lam Markmann). New York: Grove Press.

Ferber, Illit. 2013. *Philosophy and Melancholy: Benjamin's Early Reflections on Theater and Language*. Stanford: Stanford University Press.

Hegel, G.W.F. 2010. *Phänomenologie des Geistes*. Köln: Anaconda.

Horkheimer, Max, and Theodor Adorno. 1972. *Dialectic of Enlightenment* (English transl. by John Cumming). New York: Seabury Press.

Hundt-Radowsky, Hartwig von. 2011 (1819). "The Jewish Mirror" (English transl.). In: Mendes-Flohr and Reinharz 2011. 288–289.

Kafka, Franz. 1977. *Letters to Friends, Family, and Editors* (English transl. by Richard Winston and Clara Winston). New York: Schocken.

Kafka, Franz. 1991. *The Blue Octavo Notebooks* (English transl. by Ernst Kaiser and Eithne Wilkins), ed. Max Brod. Cambridge: Exact Change.

Kant, Immanuel. 1996. "The Conflict of the Faculties." In: idem, *Religion and Rational Theology* (English transl. by Allen W. Wood and George di Giovanni). Cambridge, UK–New York: Cambridge University Press.

Löwy, Michael. 2005. *Fire Alarm: Reading Walter Benjamin's 'On the Concept of History'* (English transl. from the French by Chris Turner). London–New York: Verso.
Marcus, Laura, and Lynda Nead (eds.). 1998. *The Actuality of Walter Banjamin*. London: Lawrence & Wishart.
Mendes-Flohr, Paul. 1989. *From Mysticism to Dialogue: Martin Buber's Transformation of German Social Thought*. Detroit: Wayne State University Press.
Mendes-Flohr, Paul, and Jehuda Reinharz. 2011. *The Jew in the Modern World: A Documentary History*. 3rd edition, New York: Oxford University Press.
Rose, Gillian. 1998. "Walter Benjamin – Out of the Sources of Modern Judaism." In: Marcus and Nead 1998. 85–117.
Simmel, Georg. 1971. "The Stranger." In: idem, *On Individuality and Social Forms: Selected Writings*, ed. Donald N. Levine. Chicago: University of Chicago Press. 143–149.
Slezkine, Yuri. 2004. *The Jewish Century*. Princeton: Princeton University Press.
Strauss, Leo. 1953. *Natural Right and History*. Chicago: University of Chicago Press
Strauss, Leo. 1965. *Spinoza's Critique of Religion*. New York: Schocken.
Strauss, Leo. 1993. *Faith and Political Philosophy: The Correspondence between Leo Strauss and Eric Voegelin, 1934–1964*, ed. and English transl. by Peter Emberley and Barry Cooper. University Park, PA: Pennsylvania State University Press.
Veblen, Thorstein. 1998 (1919). "The Intellectual Pre-eminence of Jews in Modern Europe." In: idem, *Essays in Our Changing Order*, ed. Leon Ardzrooni. New Brunswick, NJ: Transaction Press.
Werblowsky, R.J. Zwi. 1976. *Beyond Tradition and Modernity: Changing Religions in a Changing World*. London: Athlone Press.
Wiehn, Erhard R. 1992. "Zu Martin Bubers Sammlung 'Die Gesellschaft': Ein fast vergessenes Stück Soziologiegeschichte in Erinnerung an den 25. Todestag ihres Herausgebers." In: Carsten Klingermann, Michael Neumann, Karl-Siegbert Rehberg, Ilja Srubar and Erhard Stölting (eds.), *Jahrbuch für Soziologiegeschichte 1991*. 183–208.
Zunz, Leopold. 2011 (1819). "Features of the Jews to Be Corrected" (English transl. of idem, "Entwurf der an den Juden zu verbesserden Gegenstaende," December 15, 1819). In: Mendes-Flohr and Reinharz 2011. 287–288.

Israel Gershoni

# Depoliticization and Denationalization of Religion: Aḥmad Luṭfī al-Sayyid and the Relocation of Islam in Modern Life

> It is a most striking feature of Kant's philosophy that although he is deeply-versed in mathematical physics, and strides forward in the central tradition of science-and-mathematics-based philosophy exemplified by Descartes, Leibniz, Locke and Hume, and sticks strictly to its rules – that is to say, he relies solely on argument, appeals only to rational criteria, rejects any appeal to faith or revelation – he arrives at conclusions which are in line not just with religion but with the more mystical forms of religious belief, Eastern as well as Western.
> Brian Magee on Immanuel Kant[1]

## Introduction: Visiting the Tomb of the Prophet in Medina

In the spring of 1911, Abū ʿAlī al-Sayyid asked his son Aḥmad Luṭfī al-Sayyid[2] (January 1872 – March 1963) to accompany him on a pilgrimage to Medina. It was the father's intention to fulfill his dream of visiting the tomb of the Prophet Muḥammad. The son, Luṭfī, was skeptical and uncertain. His father's request did not necessarily accord with Luṭfī's plans, or his worldview. Most likely, he did not attach particular importance to the idea of the pilgrimage. In his many writings leading up to this event, Luṭfī had not expressed a wish to make the journey to the tomb of the Prophet, or to make the *Ḥajj*. But his father urged him, and he accepted.

When Luṭfī attempted to explain, both to himself and to his readers, the meaning of his decision, he did not rely on religious or legal *sharʿī* substantiation in the execution of this fundamental Islamic commandment. He justified his choice, rather, as the fulfillment of another commandment, that of "honor thy

*Acknowledgment:* This article was generously supported by the Israel Science Foundation, grant number 185/17.

1 Magee 1987:185.

2 See the reference list at the end of this article for abbreviations of the titles of works by Aḥmad Luṭfī al-Sayyid. His articles in *Al-Jarīda* are cited by their titles and publication years and by their page ranges in the volumes in which they are collected. All other works are cited in the author-date style used throughout this volume.

https://doi.org/10.1515/9783110723984-006

father." It was Luṭfī's great respect and love for his father that tipped the scales and influenced his decision. He was convinced of his responsibility to honor his loving and devoted father's request, just as he would expect similar devotion and love from his own children. As he honestly depicted, the strongest feelings "that stirred [his] soul on the eve of this journey" were derived from the anxiety of the "separation from his children."[3] From his office in downtown Cairo in June 1911, Luṭfī said goodbye to his two sons and his young daughter as they embraced him with tears of worry and love before he set off on his journey. Luṭfī took advantage of this opportunity to describe in detail the "feelings of love between fathers and sons in the pain of separation, longing for reunion." He admitted frankly: "I am one of the people who gives top priority to the emotional proximity between fathers and sons." Thus, on the eve of their departure, it was not the resting place of the Prophet that inspired him, but rather his strong feelings of familial affection and the experience of separation, which ensured at its conclusion a renewed connection of love with his children, his spouse and his family, and with his home and his homeland.

At the time of the journey, the differences between Luṭfī and his father were unbridgeable. Abū ʿAlī was an unknown *ʿumda* of the village of Barqayn (*shaykh al-balad*, the village shaykh) in the province (*mudīriyya*) of Daqahliyya, where Luṭfī was born and spent his childhood.[4] Luṭfī, by contrast, was already a recognized public and political figure – the ideologue of the Party of the Nation (Ḥizb al-Umma) and the editor of its daily journal, *Al-Jarīda*. He had moved to the capital, Cairo, where he became a prominent public intellectual whose opinions and perspectives were heard and were read daily by tens of thousands of readers. Later referred to by his disciples with great admiration as "the teacher of the generation" (*ustādh al-jīl*), Luṭfī, whose remarkable career spanned six decades of the twentieth century, is rightly identified as one of the most original and brightest intellectuals to emerge in Egypt in the early 1900s.[5]

Luṭfī's father, who was very proud of his son, may have thought it fitting that Luṭfī, who had by that time already visited Europe, the Middle East and Turkey and had mastered English and French, should accompany him on this journey. Despite his Western education, which had given him a strong European

---

**3** "Usbūʿ fī al-Madīna al-Munawwara" (1911), part 1, *MN*, I:229–230; see also *QH*:121–123.

**4** *QH*:18–20.

**5** For more details see *ibid.*:21–143, 160–200; and Ḥamza 1958–1963, esp. VI:543–785. Volume VI of Ḥamza's monumental work is devoted entirely to Aḥmad Luṭfī al-Sayyid's thought and to *Al-Jarīda*. See also: Ahmed 1960:44–112; al-Najjār 1963 and 1965; Afaf Luṭfī al-Sayyid 1968:155–208; Wendell 1972:200–313; al-Shalaq 1979; and Sharaf 2002.

orientation, Luṭfī never repudiated his traditional religious background. His primary education was in a traditional village *kuttāb*, where he excelled in the study of Islam, culminating in his ability, as a child, to recite the entire Qurʾān by heart. Naturally, his father wanted him to pursue further education at al-Azhar. He believed that his son would be a worthy *ʿālim*. But a turning point in the boy's life, under the influence of family friend Ibrahim Adham Pasha, governor of Daqahliyya, led to his decision to continue his education at the al-Mansura government school. He then enrolled in the Khedivial Secondary School in Cairo. From there, his path as an outstanding student led directly to higher study at the prestigious Khedivial School of Law in Cairo and to a respectable position as a public prosecutor in the Colonial British Egyptian Ministry of Justice.[6] From the beginning of 1907, with his resignation from this post and his decision to act as the editor of *Al-Jarīda*, Luṭfī began to see his life's mission as a large-scale project of translating and domesticating the Enlightenment and modernity into Egyptian politics, society and culture. This would be a vehicle for freeing Egypt from British colonial rule, preparing it for independence and sovereignty, and reshaping its imagined national community as exclusively Egyptian.[7]

Strange though it seems, given that, at the time, transport to the Hijaz and back to Cairo would have taken several long weeks, father and son decided to settle for a pilgrimage to the tomb of the Prophet in "the holy city of Medina," and they never reached Mecca to fulfill the *Ḥajj*. It appears to have been Luṭfī who determined the route. As he describes in his travel diaries, they journeyed to Palestine via Jaffa and then to Damascus, and then, via the Hijaz railway, they traveled south to Tabūk on the way to Medina. The father, a traditional religious man on what would have been his first journey outside of Egypt, must surely have expected to reach Mecca and carry out his religious obligation. And so it appears that Luṭfī must specifically have refused, and the father was forced to acquiesce. Luṭfī's records, however, do not provide clear evidence for this conclusion, and he does not explain the decision. In any case, it is clear that they visited the tomb of the Prophet, spent nearly a week in Medina and then returned directly to Cairo.[8]

Luṭfī documented his journey in real time and again in his memoirs. He published a "thick description" in *Al-Jarīda* in the summer of 1911, in a series of six articles entitled "A Week in Illuminated Medina" (*Usbūʿ fī al-Madīna al-Munawwara*).[9] As Luṭfī colorfully described, when the train from Tabūk was approaching

---

**6** *QH*:25–29.
**7** *QH*:42–47.
**8** "Usbūʿ fī al-Madīna al-Munawwara," Part 1 (1911), *MN*, I:229–232.
**9** "Usbūʿ fī al-Madīna al-Munawwara" (1911), *MN*, I:229–251; *QH*:121–130.

Medina, he felt a surge of awe and transcendence as they entered the city. His soul "stormed and stirred," inspired by "the memory of ancient Arab glory." The aura and rays of "light flowing from Medina" determinedly steered him and the other travelers into the special holy atmosphere. The next day, when he and his father entered the sanctuary in the tomb of the Prophet, Luṭfī was thrilled and excited. Feelings of reverence and awe flooded through him. The silence that surrounded the holy place accentuated the splendor and glory of "the burial place of the Prophet, the place of death of the great man, the powerful Prophet, and the noble apostle." Standing before the holy sanctuary, Luṭfī felt "submissive" and "lowly" as he beheld "the tomb whose splendor and glory has no limits," a place "incomparable" to any other in the history of humankind.

Muḥammad's historical greatness is reflected in the restrained but impressive description. "Those who believe in Muḥammad, and myself included, rightly see him as the greatest human being. Even those who do not believe in him cannot deny that he was the noblest and most enlightened among men." Luṭfī recalls the greatness of Muḥammad, who "made the *hijra* alone with a few Companions" to the desert of Medina, convinced of God's revelation to him, with new faith and tidings for humanity. He stuck to God's mission and accomplished it against all odds. The respected elite of Medina, "men of wealth and prestige and military might," did not trust him, nor did they help him. On the contrary, they shut him out and rejected his faith. Yet, despite this brutal denial, "Allah gave him knowledge, wisdom, prophecy and a mission, and he was victorious. After all, there is no victory but by the might of Allah." The extraordinary power of Muḥammad was embodied in his virtuous leadership, the mission he received from God, his persistence in his goals and his determination to succeed. [10]

Notwithstanding these expressions of emotion and spiritual elevation, there is still something cool, rational, restrained and remote in Luṭfī's descriptions of his visit to the tomb of the Prophet. Luṭfī's Muḥammad comes across as a major historical and cultural hero, an original and innovative reformer with the loftiest ethical and moral standards. He is less a "religious prophet" in the orthodox sense than the precursor and founder of a new religion and law (*sharīʿa*) to guide humanity; less a messenger to whom Allah revealed himself, whom all Muslims must follow and embody in their lives, than a great social and political leader who fomented a social and political revolution that inspired humanity at large. That the journey to Medina did not continue on to Mecca and to the *Ḥajj* teaches

**10** "Usbūʿ fī al-Madīna al-Munawwara," Parts 2 and 3 (1911), esp. *MN*, I:234–237; *QH*, pp. 121–130.

us a great deal about Luṭfī's approach. In his refusal to make the *Ḥajj*, Luṭfī, albeit implicitly, expresses a strong opinion about the status of traditional, legal Islam.[11]

Moreover, the scenery of the journey through the Hijaz to Medina and back again was largely foreign to Luṭfī. He was quick to compare every personal or collective "Arab" mode of life that he encountered or observed to their parallels in Egyptian life, highlighting the foreignness and distance that he felt in relation to what he saw. The "Arab" was not "Egyptian," and the "Egyptian" was not "Arab." Luṭfī describes the anonymous inhabitants of the desert in the "Lands of the Arabian Peninsula" (*bilād al-ʿarab*) with a certain admiration for their unique characteristics of "bravery," "heroism" and "honor," but he also finds them remote from the "advanced" modern characteristics of the Egyptians. He dedicates an entire article to describing "the women in the regions of the Arabian Peninsula," the Arab Bedouin women. Even as he praises them for their "high moral standards," their "independence and determination" and their role in "educating [their] children to do good," he highlights major differences between them and Egyptian women in lifestyle, behavioral norms and dress fashions. Noting that the Egyptian women were much closer in style to European women and to the new, modern model of education, he concludes: "the Arab women lag behind significantly in education and knowledge, and are backward compared to those in Egypt or Turkey." Even if Luṭfī was generous in his flattering observations of the "Arabs" and "their desert lifestyle," he clearly found them foreign, different and far removed from his native Egypt.[12]

## Religion in the Age of Enlightenment and Nationalism

Luṭfī's description of his visit to Medina seems accurately to embody his attitude toward religion in general and toward Islam in particular. By the summer of 1911, his worldview, as editor of *Al-Jarīda*, had already crystallized. Within his modernist agenda, Islam was newly defined in terms of Enlightenment and nationalism. Unlike his father, Luṭfī placed himself among the founders of the "Renaissance/Awakening" (*nahḍa*) and of a new "modernity," which he identified with "the Enlightenment." His favorite terms were "civilization/to become civilized" (*tamaddun/mutammaddin*), "progress/advancement" (*irtiqāʾ*) and "freedom/liberty" (*ḥurriyya*).

11 "Usbūʿ fī al-Madīna al-Munawwara," Part 3 (1911), *MN*, I:236–240.
12 "Usbūʿ fī al-Madīna al-Munawwara," Part 4 (1911), *MN*, I:241–245.

With this mission and self-image, Luṭfī effectively cut himself off from his father's generation, which he considered outdated, traditionalist and rural. His education in civil institutions, particularly the Khedivial School of Law, had torn him away from that generation and set him in the new, modern generation of Cairo's intellectual urban elite. Luṭfī was fully aware of and comfortable with this profound transformation. In 1907, when he became the editor of *Al-Jarīda*, his life's mission became clear to him: He gave everything he had to become the reproducer and ultimate translator of the Enlightenment in Egypt. He viewed himself as the prime initiator of the process of "Egyptianization (*tamṣīr*) of the Enlightenment," which was promoting "the new civilization" (*al-tamaddun al-ḥadīth*). Luṭfī's intellectual cohort viewed him as one of the most prominent Egyptian intellectuals to identify with the ideas, values and institutions of the European Enlightenment. He invested great efforts in explaining these values to his countrymen and in integrating and implementing them in the local Egyptian Islamic environment.[13] This role required him to reiterate his perspective on religion in general and on Islam in particular. Stubbornly and with admirable perseverance, he repeatedly attempted to answer the essential questions: What is the place of religion in the modern world? What is the role of God in the age of science and reason? How can we redefine Islam to facilitate *tamaddun*, *irtiqā'* and *ḥurriyya*?

Any attempt to understand Luṭfī's position on religion must address his stance on nationalism. In all of his writings, he started from the assumption that the modern era, in European and non-European societies, was characterized by integration and implementation of the Enlightenment, and that the central agent of translation was nationalism and the nation. This was a global process to which Egypt had to adapt. Therefore, "the Egyptian nation" (*al-umma al-miṣriyya*) must, in every respect and norm, replace "the Islamic nation" (*al-umma al-islāmiyya*) as the sole communal identity for all the inhabitants of the Nile Valley. It was the Egyptian *umma* that must guide the conduct of Egyptian life in its political, social, economic, cultural, artistic and ethical aspects. The Egyptian nation was formed by conscious acts of "Egyptian nationalism" (*al-qawmiyya al-miṣriyya*) and "Egyptian patriotism" (*al-waṭaniyya al-miṣriyya*). These forces framed the minds and actions of "the Egyptians who strive to establish for themselves an independent and sovereign nation, free and modern."[14]

By its very nature, modern nationalism is a secular, post-religious nationalism; it is not and cannot be based on religion. On both discursive and practical

13 *QH*:21–157; Wendell 1972:201–293.

14 "al-Jāmi'a al-Miṣriyya [1]" (1909), *MN*, I:170–172; "al-Jāmi'a al-Miṣriyya [2]" (1909), *MN*, I:183.

levels, nationalism undertakes the management of politics, society and culture, thereby emptying religion of its role in all these spheres of life. Luṭfī identified the concepts of Enlightenment/civilization (*tamaddun*), progress/advancement (*taraqqī*, *irtiqāʾ*), science, reason and freedom/liberty (*ḥurriyya*) with nationalism. This liberal nationalism translates and domesticates ideas of Enlightenment and modernity and makes them both local and Egyptian. The first mission of the enlightened thinker was to explain and justify why religion in general, and Islam in particular, as the hegemonic religion of the Egyptian people, could no longer provide a basis for the nation's new life, nor could it function as a modern collective identity.[15]

Luṭfī's efforts to dismantle Islam's national and political meanings and contents often turned into sharp criticism of attempts to blur religion and nationalism. To him, the claim that religion in general, and Islam in particular, could offer a social and political agenda posed a threat to nationalism and so also to modernity and Enlightenment. The effort to preserve religion as a collective political system to compete with nationalism seemed to him meaningless, anachronistic, anti-modern and therefore worthy of rejection. Luṭfī devoted many articles to the elimination or neutralization of religion and Islam in the context of nationalism. For example, in "al-Miṣriyya" (Egyptianism/Egyptianness), a typical article on the subject published in January 1913, Luṭfī reiterates his liberal nationalist doctrine of "who is Egyptian" as well as his determined opposition to any attempt at mixing religious identity with Egyptian national identity. Rejecting any definition of "Egyptianness" based on race, language or place of origin, he declares that religion, too, has no role in the design of a modern national identity. "An Egyptian," he asserts, is simply "someone who knows no homeland other than Egypt."[16] If one resides in Egypt and works willingly for its benefit and towards its greater good (*manfaʿa*), whatever his/her origin, ethnicity, religion or mother tongue, then s/he is a patriotic Egyptian (on the level of *waṭaniyya*) and an Egyptian nationalist (on the level of *qawmiyya*).

Hence, those who reside in Egypt and assume that they can declare loyalty to "two homelands" – if they allow themselves "another homeland" or seek an identity outside of the Nile Valley – they are "far from being Egyptian in the true sense of the term." Luṭfī's meaning is clear. Those "of us" who believe that they can split their collective identity between their Egyptian and their Islamic or Ottoman (or Arab) identity, and so enjoy both the "Egyptian homeland" and the

**15** "Taḍāmununā" (1913), *TA*:65–68; "Miṣriyyatunā" (1913) , *TA*:69–71; "al-Taqlīd" (1913) , *TA*:80–83; "Ilā al-shabība: al-iḍṭirāb fī al-raʾy al-ʿāmm" (1912), *MN*, I:307–312, *MB*:106–112.
**16** "al-Miṣriyya" (1913), *TA*:72–74.

"Ottoman" or "Islamic" homeland, assuming there is no contradiction between them – they are not Egyptian patriots. Their nationalism is partially or completely invalid, because it mixes religious identity with national political identity.[17] In an early article, from 1908, Luṭfī set down the general rule that Egyptian "national solidarity" was "propelled by the force of patriotism and national benefits" (*ʿāmil al-waṭaniyya wa al-manfaʿa al-qawmiyya*) and not by any other religious, racial or ethnic factor. Hence, he declares, "politics (*siyāsa*) that is not founded on nationalism and utility has a flawed and distorted value ... which does not advance the nation in any sense toward true modernity/civilization."[18] Only nationalism, that is, Egyptianism, has political content and can create a political culture and a non-religious, political government that guarantees civilization, freedom, progress and prosperity.

Based on these assumptions, Luṭfī maintained his attacks on the view, still widespread within the Egyptian public, that Islam was nationalist, patriotic and a legitimate framework for political identity in the modern age. There was a specific historical context to his reproaches, which started appearing in the first issues of *Al-Jarīda* in the spring of 1907 but escalated toward the end of the 1912–1914 period. They were directed particularly against the traditional *ʿulamā* and other orthodox and conservative forces surrounding the Egyptian Khedive ʿAbbās Ḥilmī II. The Khedive, a Turkish speaker and the key representative of the Ottoman Egyptian ruling elite, who maintained and defended his Ottoman identity and presented himself as an Egyptian-Ottoman ruler, became a constant target of criticism by Luṭfī and *Al-Jarīda*. Luṭfī attacked ʿAbbās's "tyranny," which, to him, was intimately connected with the autocratic Ottoman political culture.[19]

Simultaneously, Luṭfī targeted leaders and activists of the Nationalist Party (Al-Ḥizb al-Waṭanī) for criticism. These Egyptian nationalists (*al-waṭaniyyūn*) aimed to design an Islamic-Ottoman Egyptian national identity. As they saw it, their brand of nationalism could function tactically as a vehicle for the Egyptian-Ottoman anticolonial struggle against the British. On a more essential level, they viewed Egypt as an Islamic land in which the majority of people were Muslims. Hence, for them, Islam was a central component of the Egyptian national identity and of the political culture of the Egyptian state, and the Egyptian *ʿumma* was an integral part of the Islamic-Ottoman state and cultural framework. This concept

17 "Ilā al-shabība: al-iḍṭirāb fī al-raʾy al-ʿāmm" (1912), *MN*, I:307–312, *MB*:106–112.
18 Public address in Alexandria (1908), *SM*:33.
19 See, e.g., Editorial (1907), *SM*:57–68; and "Siyāsat al-Wifāq" (1908), *SM*:137–139. For a more general view of Luṭfī's negative attitude to the Khedive ʿAbbas Hilmi II see his early series of articles, "al-Umma wa-al-Ḥukūma" (1907–1908), *MB*:28–62. See also *QH*:48–50.

of an Islamic Egyptian nationalism was formulated by the party's founder and first leader, Muṣṭafā Kāmil, as early as 1900–1908. After Kāmil's death in 1908, the new party leaders, Muḥammad Farīd and ʿAbd al-ʿAzīz Jāwīsh, pursued a more rigorous Islamic nationalist anticolonial agenda. They advocated endorsement of the Ottoman-Turkish state and, with the outbreak of World War I, supported and actively participated in its fight against the British. These later leaders and spokesmen of the Nationalist Party buttressed the Egyptian religious nationalist ideology, often by way of populist or demagogic propaganda.[20]

In the face of these strong domestic forces, Luṭfī al-Sayyid braced himself with courage and determination. He was not above using aggressive language. "There are those who claim that the Islamic land is the homeland of all Muslims (*bi-anna arḍ al-islām waṭan li-kull al-muslimīn*)," he declared. Those who make this claim, he continued, base their "nationalism" on

> an imperialistic principle (*qāʿida istiʿmāriyya*) enjoyed by any imperialist nation *(umma istiʿmāriyya)* committed to expanding its territories and its influence ... a principle that is easily consistent with the strong occupying race that colonizes lands in the name of religion.

And this "while depriving the national rights of all the inhabitants of the colonized lands."[21] In other words, the "imperialist principle" underlying the argument that the Islamic world is the homeland of all Muslims, and Egypt is therefore not a distinct nation and a distinctive homeland in its own right ("Egypt is the homeland of every Muslim"), is the same principle that guided the "Western imperialism" currently colonizing the "Lands of the East." Under the guise of this distorted principle, Western imperialists repressed and subjugated the people of the East to serve colonial needs and interests.[22] Luṭfī repeatedly explained that the "imperialist principle" which holds that religion is nationalism "is no longer legitimate and is liable to disappear. Because it is no longer consistent with the current modern reality of Islamic nations and their aspirations." He reminded his readers that the notion of Islam as a land that incorporates all the believers into one unified identity had faded away and disappeared in light of the profound structural change produced by modern conditions.

> This [obsolete] principle had already been replaced by the sole school of thought best suited to the aspirations of every Eastern (and Islamic) nation with a specifically defined

**20** Goldschmidt 1968. For a more general view, see Toledano 2015.
**21** "al-Miṣriyya" (1913), *TA*:72; "ʿAlaykum Anfusakum" (1909), *MN*, I:164–166; "Ilā al-shabība: Gharaḍ al-Umma huwa al-Istiqlāl" (1912), *MN*, I:316.
**22** "al-Miṣriyya" (1913), *TA*:72.

> homeland; and this school is exclusively nationalism (*madhab al-waṭaniyya*) and none other. "Pan-Islamic unity" (*al-jāmiʿa al-islāmiyya*) no longer has the right to exist; its time has passed, and it has been replaced by "Egyptian unity" (*al-jāmiʿa al-miṣriyya*), the genuine unity of modern man and society. Hence, our Egyptianness (*miṣriyyatunā*) obligates us exclusively to our homeland as the sole focus of our attention (*qiblatunā*).[23]

Moreover, Luṭfī, contrary to the image of him described by many scholars, developed a cohesive and sometimes assertive anticolonial stance, albeit framed in restrained and moderate language. More than many of his contemporaries, he was entirely aware of Egypt's colonial status. He had learned the extent of the British colonial power in Egypt, and, based on an in-depth analysis of its character, he predicted that it would remain in Egypt for many years to come. He understood well that the European Enlightenment project, imported and translated to the local Egyptian reality, was taking place at a time when Europe, particularly the Great Powers, England and France, were conducting brutal imperialist attacks on the "East," in Egypt and other parts of the Arab Middle East, Asia and Africa.[24] According to Luṭfī, one of the major aims of the colonizers was to prove to the colonized (and to themselves) that, by virtue of their being Muslims, Egyptians were inherently unable to emulate the values, norms and practices of the European Enlightenment. Here Luṭfī depicts colonialism as reactionary, regressive and racist. Luṭfī and other local "enlightened liberal intellectuals" aimed to demonstrate that the achievement of modernity and nationalist goals demanded freeing the colonized people (including themselves) from religion and traditional Islam, or at least neutralization of its role in the modern experience. The European colonialists, however, argued that this was a futile endeavor. Enlightenment, in their view, could be realized only in Christian Europe, where the religious conditions were well suited to Enlightenment values.

In many of his writings, Luṭfī accused the colonialist powers of condemning and attacking Islam as a negative and archaic ideological, institutional and practical system, thus blocking Muslims from coping with and accepting modernity in productive ways. Luṭfī discovered the origins of this reprehensible and stereotypical representation of Islam in early writings of Enlightenment philosophy, particularly those of Montesquieu. This influential French thinker, whom Luṭfī admired in many ways, went astray in his racist and essentialist attitude toward Islam and the East, and in his references to "substantive despotism" as deriving from Islam. According to Montesquieu, Luṭfī claims, "the Christian religion advances and strengthens the parliamentary rule of law, while the Moḥammedan

---

**23** *Ibid.*, *TA*:73–74. See also "al-Jāmiʿa al-Miṣriyya" (1909), *MN*, I:183.

**24** See, e.g., "Al-Ḥāla al-Ḥāḍira" (1908), *MB*:64–91; "Naḥnu wa al-Istiqlāl" (1908), *SM*:121–125.

religion strengthens authoritarian rule (*al-ḥukūma al-istibdādiyya*)."[25] In *The Spirit of the Laws*, as Luṭfī points out, Montesquieu argued that

> The moderate government is better suited to the Christian religion, and despotic government to Mohammedanism. ... The Christian religion is remote from pure despotism, and [its leaders] are more disposed to give laws to themselves and more capable of feeling that they cannot do everything .... The [Christian] prince counts on his subjects, and the subjects on the prince."

Islam, by contrast, encourages "despotic government," and its leaders "constantly kill or are killed" by their political rivals.[26]

Luṭfī challenged this condescending attitude and set out to prove its simple-mindedness, racism and ignorance. That the church, over hundreds of years and "really up until the last century, promoted autocratic absolutist governments" demonstrates that Montesquieu was wrong. Even the French royal House of Bourbon rested on the divine Christian right to power, which supported an absolute monarchy.[27] More generally, in Europe, until very recently, "the king ruled in the name of God and not in the name of the nation; his governmental authority was derived from God." But even after the French Revolution and the advance of modernity in Christian Europe, the political use of religion to impose legitimacy and power remained. As Luṭfī asserts, "Some European statesmen today [in the era of European imperialism] exploit religion as a means to achieve and realize political goals and ambitions." For him, "this attitude is based on false assumptions and is a misleading path." [28]

Luṭfī found in Voltaire a legitimate authority to emphasize his point. Voltaire viciously attacked the absolutism of the Bourbon monarchy and showed that the Christian religion, on which its legitimacy was based, did not promote the "rule of justice" but rather was an obstacle to its establishment.[29] It was Christianity, then, and not Islam, that legitimized the regime of absolute monarchy. Moreover, Luṭfī was convinced that specific historical circumstances were responsible for the emergence of dictatorial governments. They were not directly connected to religion of any stripe and did not derive from any religious instruction or commandment, Christian or Muslim.[30]

---

**25** "Al-Inklīz fī Miṣr aw Intiqād Kitāb *Miṣr al-Ḥadītha*, Ta'līf al-Lūrd Krūmar" (1908), *SM*:110–111.
**26** Montesquieu 1889:461.
**27** "Al-Inklīz fī Miṣr aw Intiqād Kitāb *Miṣr al-Ḥadītha*, Ta'līf al-Lūrd Krūmar" (1908), *SM*:110.
**28** *Ibid.*
**29** *Ibid.*; "Ilā al-shabība: al-iḍṭirāb fī al-ra'y al-ʿāmm" (1912), *MN*, I:308–311, *MB*:107–110.
**30** "Al-Inklīz fī Miṣr aw Intiqād Kitāb *Miṣr al-Ḥadītha*, Ta'līf al-Lūrd Krūmar" (1908), *SM*:109–112. See also Luṭfī's public address in Alexandria (1908), *SM*:30–33.

European colonialism developed and reinforced an anti-Islamic ideology that rested on unfounded prejudices and loathsome stereotypes, which it recreated in the contemporary imperialist context. Beyond its perception of Islam as promoting and propagating autocratic rule, colonialism also portrayed Muslims in Egypt as "religious fanatics" who intended to create an Islamic front to challenge the Christian West. It was, in fact, the European colonial powers who had "invented" pan-Islamism, which had no meaningful hold in Egypt or in the Ottoman Arab world. This "purely colonialist" invention was designed to create a negative, fanatical and demonic image of the Islamic community as obsessed with unifying the Muslims against the West, for the sake of inflaming violence and perpetrating xenophobic, anti-European and anti-Enlightenment sentiments.[31] Even some European intellectuals and journalists were involved in circulating and legitimizing this deplorable image of the Muslims, including Egyptians.

In an early article, from May 1907, Luṭfī alleged that "European" (particularly British and French) statesmen, in their effort "to preserve the occupation forever," claimed that the "built-in defect of Egypt is that it is an Islamic nation." For this reason alone, unlike the Christian lands of the Balkans, it was not suitable for self-governance or independence. These colonialists "imagined" Islamic Egypt as part of the "pan-Islamic community" in order to perpetuate further colonization of the Nile Valley. Luṭfī challenged this logic, sarcastically noting the absence, in the colonial lexicon, of claims to a "Christian union" or references to "Pan-Christianity." Just as there is no "Christian union," he declares, there is also no "Islamic union." "Pan-Islamism" is a colonial construct aimed at serving specific imperial political and economic interests, "a true expression of European politics in the East today" and "a screen designed to cover their [Imperialist] actions in the East."[32]

The British colonial rulers in Egypt shared the blame for the creation and dissemination of pan-Islamic images within the Egyptian public. Luṭfī blamed Lord Cromer, the British Consul and Agent in Egypt from 1883 to 1907, and other senior British civil servants who implemented the colonial regime for their role in circulating these negative images in order to facilitate the institutionalization and perpetuation of British hegemony in the Nile Valley. Cromer's 1908 book *Modern Egypt*, published after he stepped down from his post, falls into stereotypes and prejudices, supposedly based on experiences he had amassed in Egypt. Luṭfī, who during Cromer's rule had accorded him a certain credit and even praised him for his accomplishments in the fields of finance and economics,

**31** "Taqrīr al-Lūrd Krūmar" (1907), *SM*:96–99; *QH*:69–72.
**32** *Ibid.*, esp. *SM*:99.

was shocked by the extent of the racist, colonialist, anti-Islamic (and, I would add, Orientalist) attitude revealed in the book and did not mince words in criticizing it. Cromer, he charged, was a fraud and an enemy of Egyptian society who had emasculated and distorted its image and impugned its "Islamic mentality."[33] But Cromer reflected a more general British colonialist outlook. The British colonial authorities, to Luṭfī's mind, deployed the images of Egyptian Muslims as "fanatics," "pan-Islamists" or "advocates of autocratic absolutism" as a weapon of legitimacy for their reprehensible actions. Why must they dominate and enslave the Egyptians? Why did they refrain from promoting self-rule in Egypt by Egyptians for Egyptians? Why did they not give the Egyptian nation the independence, freedom and sovereignty it deserved; and why did they not encourage the emergence of a parliamentary constitutional government, progressive modern education and an independent economy? From this perspective, Luṭfī claims, the Egyptians "among us" who mixed nationalism and religion and pined for an Islamic Egyptian national identity were allies and collaborators of colonialism. His staunch opposition to pan-Islamism was thus part and parcel of his critique of colonialism. This was Luṭfī's weapon in his struggle for the de-colonialization of Egypt and other lands in Asia and Africa.[34]

In sum, Luṭfī declared, objective observation of the Egyptian reality clearly indicates that "pan-Islamic association (*al-jāmiʿa al-islāmiyya*) is totally foreign to Egyptians, baseless ... without concrete existence ... [and] it has no impact on Egypt or on any place outside of Egypt."[35] Elsewhere, he characterizes notions of "pan-Islamic association" and other sentiments of Islamic unity as "delusions and fantasies" (*awhām wa-khayālāt*), as "this impossible association (*hādhihi al-jāmiʿa al-mustaḥīla*), since it is based in religion," or more simply as "the imaginary Islamic association" (*al-jāmiʿa al-islāmiyya al-mawhūma*).[36] All these "pan-religious delusions" are fake constructs of external colonialist interests, supported by domestic Islamic militancy. As Luṭfī sarcastically put it in a 1907 article, "pan-Islamism is a fairy tale (*khurāfa*) invented by the ingenuity of a [London] *Times* correspondent in Vienna."[37] Five years later, he wrote: "The history and the natural condition of humanity determine that benefits and interests (*manfaʿa*,

---

**33** "Al-Inklīz fī Miṣr aw Intiqād Kitāb *Miṣr al-Ḥadītha*, Taʾlīf al-Lūrd Krūmar" (1908), *SM*:106–112; "al-Raʾy al-ʿāmm" (1908), *MN*, I:28–32; see also *QH*:64–68; "al-Lūrd al-Krūmar Imām al-Taʾrīkh" (1907), *SM*:69–74; "al-Siyāsa al-Inklīziyya" (1907), *SM*:75–76.

**34** "Al-Ḥāla al-Ḥāḍira" (1908); public address in Alexandria (1908), *SM*:7–38; "Al-Inklīz fī Miṣr aw Intiqād Kitāb *Miṣr al-Ḥadītha*, Taʾlīf al-Lūrd Krūmar" (1908), *SM*:109–112.

**35** "Taqrīr al-Lūrd Krūmar" (1907), *SM*:99.

**36** "Aʿmālunā" (1913), esp. *MB*:217.

**37** "Taqrīr al-Lūrd Krūmar" (1907), *SM*:100.

pl. *manāfiʿ*) are the sole foundation that unifies people into a shared collective." These "basic elements" cancel out the "unity of race or religion." Only nationalism that is based solely on "cooperation over interests and utilities," that rejects every form of "pan-religious unity," can be considered appropriate, enlightened, modern and progressive, "and therein is the sole base for political action."[38]

Luṭfī's rejection of "pan-Islamic unity" was not only outward-oriented; he did not singularly fault western colonialism for the perpetuation of this concept. The idea also had supporters at home in Egypt. Even if it did not express itself as "pan-Islam" (*ban Islam*), the sentiment still existed as an Egyptian-Ottoman discourse and practice in Ottoman Egypt. More specifically, Luṭfī identified the "Ottoman Islamic identity" that claimed the adherence of many Egyptians, both elites and on the street, as a direct threat to "Egyptianism" (*al-miṣriyya*) and "Egyptian nationalism" (*al-qawmiyya al-miṣriyya*). In the context of the first and second decades of the twentieth century, Luṭfī was not wrong. The Ottoman Empire was the de-facto ruler of Egypt. Luṭfī defined its status as the "legal authority" (*al-sulṭa al-sharʿiyya*) in Egypt, as opposed to the British colonial regime, which he termed "the acting authority" (*al-sulṭa al-fiʿiliyya*).[39] Egypt's Islamic Ottoman identity was not only shared and accepted but also reinforced by the official and public anti-colonial struggle and the belief that only with the help of the Ottoman state could Egypt succeed in removing the British colonial occupying power.

Muṣṭafā Kāmil and his followers in the Nationalist Party had already begun to develop and institutionalize this view at the beginning of the century. It was strengthened further after the signing of the 1904 Entente Cordiale between Britain and France on the distribution of colonies and areas of influence and occupation in Africa. The Egyptians' bitter disappointment with "treacherous" France, and their consequent increased faith in the Ottoman Empire even under the authoritarian Sultan ʿAbd al-Ḥamīd II, became a major component in the Nationalist Party's propaganda and policies.[40] Luṭfī saw in this a dangerous misconception that confused the authentic Egyptian identity with an artificial, anachronistic Egyptian-Ottoman identity, a subject to which he devoted dozens of articles. Ottomanism, like Islamism, could no longer provide a framework for a modern collective identity. Both were archaic religious identities to which national Enlightenment had put an end. Therefore, wrote Luṭfī, "We must say that Egyptians are the original inhabitants of this Egyptian country. Every Ottoman

**38** "Ilā al-shabība: al-iḍṭirāb fī al-ra'y al-ʿāmm" (1912), *MN*, I:307–312, *MB*:106–112.
**39** Public address in Alexandria (1908), esp. *SM*:28–30.
**40** Goldschmidt 1968:317–329.

who came to settle here claimed this land as his exclusive homeland without any other additional Ottoman homelands." The Egyptian homeland is open to any migrant, but it demands of its inhabitants, old and new, "absolute loyalty to it and only to it," Luṭfī declared; "Egyptian patriotism, based on love of the homeland (*ḥubb al-waṭan*) does not accept a partner."

Members of the Ottomanist "school of thought" (that is, activists in the Nationalist Party and their supporters) took the "extremely dangerous" view that "Egypt is not only the homeland of the Egyptians but the homeland of any Muslim ... for all Muslims around the world." The collective identity of human beings, Luṭfī insisted, could not be based on "religious principles and foundations." Essential interests alone, and not religion, must form "the basis of political actions." Therefore, the duty of Egypt's inhabitants was "only to love her and her alone." Their commitment to serve Egypt's interests obviated any other obligations: "They must prove in their words and actions that they have no home other than Egypt; that they have no tribe but the Egyptians." In essence, "these are the true Egyptians."[41]

In an appeal to the "Arab immigrants" who came from the Fertile Crescent and "still liked to view themselves as belonging to the Arabian Peninsula or to [Greater] Syria or to Turkey and not to Egypt," Luṭfī called on them to abandon their previous loyalties. In turning to the communities of recent arrivals who were in the process of "becoming Egyptian" (*mutamaṣṣirūn*), he warned that they could not view Egypt as a "passing station." Egypt was not "a place of temporary work" or a mere arena for economic activity, where one could disassociate oneself from "Egyptian nationalist feelings." Calling on the immigrants "to fully adopt" Egyptian nationalism, he warned that if they came only with the goal of "using the country for economic gain," it would "be hard for Egypt to see them as Egyptians"; they could not be part of the Egyptian homeland. Luṭfī repeatedly emphasized that this Egypt-centric attitude was not intended to detract from the country's human heterogeneity or to harm any of its religious groups. On the contrary, ethnic, racial, religious and linguistic pluralism were the basis of Egyptian nationalism. Each group could maintain its distinctiveness without breaking down the element that united them: their belonging to the singular nation of Egypt. Those who did not like Egypt or work for its benefit, he maintained, "are not Egyptians and cannot be Egyptians."[42]

---

**41** "Ilā al-shabība: al-iḍṭirāb fī al-ra'y al-'āmm" (1912), *MN*, I:307–312, *MB*:108–111.

**42** "al-Miṣriyya" (1913), *TA*:73–74; "Ilā al-shabība: al-iḍṭirāb fī al-ra'y al-'āmm" (1912), *MN*, I:308–311, *MB*:108–110.

Emptying Islam of its content of nationalist collective identity meant emptying it of its social and political contents as well. Indeed, Luṭfī's national project focused on sterilizing Islam of its communal aspects: political and social, economic and cultural. Luṭfī never adopted the term "secular" (*ʿilmānī*), though it became a convention in the Arabic political vocabulary of the period. According to his enlightened worldview, Islam must be relocated within modern reality. As an admirer of Aristotle's *Politics*, and later the translator of Aristotle's works into Arabic, Luṭfī learned from the great Greek thinker that politics are not connected to religion, nor can politics be based in religion. Luṭfī expanded Aristotle's ideas, shaped by the framework of the Greek *polis*, to the territorial framework of the Egyptian nation in the projected Egyptian nation-state. In his opinion, the politics of a nation-state had to be free of religious considerations and sentiments.[43]

This secular concept took shape under the direct influence of major Enlightenment intellectuals, such as Locke, Montesquieu, Rousseau and, in the nineteenth century, Mill and Spencer. In this view, the state is organized according to the utility and interests of its citizens and endeavors to bring about maximum happiness for all its inhabitants. Religion does not determine the structure or the content, the laws or the norms, that define the operation of the state. At its core, a nation-state must be based on a constitutional parliamentary government, which inherently ensures the existence of democratically elected civil institutions. The structure of the modern state must guarantee freedom (*al-ḥurriyya*) for all its citizens and wage an uncompromising struggle against tyranny (*al-istibdād*).

Luṭfī invested much effort in elucidating the concepts of individual liberty, civic freedom, freedom of national self-determination, sovereignty and independence. The achievement of freedom requires the facilitation of free public opinion and a free press, which must, in turn, struggle to remove all forms of autocracy or authoritarianism in society, politics and culture. In all these matters related to the realization of freedom, religion plays only a marginal role or is at least relegated to a secondary position. In order to legitimize this theme in historical context, Luṭfī asserted that the authoritarian political culture that characterized Egypt for thousands of years was never based in Islam or any other religion. It predated the rise of Islam in the seventh century, had continued for many centuries thereafter and was reasserted in the modern Egyptian state established in the nineteenth century by the rule of the Khedives, and it had continued into the present with the Khedivate of ʿAbbās Ḥilmī II. Luṭfī's exhortations on freedom thus were directed against the Khedivate as much as against British colonial rule, but he emphasized

43 Aristotle 1946; "Ilā al-shabība: al-iḍṭirāb fī al-ra'y al-ʿāmm" (1912), *MN*, I:308–312, *MB*:109–111.

that this critical struggle for freedom, for liberation from the shackles both of the traditional despotism of the past and of colonialism, was not a religious Islamic struggle but a national, civil one.[44]

Another central topic that Luṭfī discussed at length was the necessity of equal status for women in modern society. His calls for "liberation of the Muslim woman" and the institutionalization of "women's rights" – to liberty and to equality with men – were in blatant defiance both of Islamic law and of popular Sufism and traditional religious practices. Indirectly, even the Coptic Christians were held responsible for their discrimination against Coptic women in Egypt. Luṭfī admired his intellectual contemporary Qāsim Amīn and saw himself and other writers in *Al-Jarīda* as preservers and nurturers of "Qāsim's heritage" of promoting Muslim women's rights to equality, freedom and unveiling, the dismantling of their seclusion and their pursuit of employment and education. Luṭfī was especially enthusiastic about Amīn's second book, *al-Mar'a al-Jadīda* (The new woman, 1901), which situated women's rights to equality among the universal human values, drawing directly upon nineteenth-century post-Enlightenment writings on the natural state of women, like men, as "free human beings." He indirectly rejected Amīn's early book *Taḥrīr al-Mar'a* (The liberation of women, 1899), and its prescribed process for changing the status of women via *ijtihād* and modern reinterpretation of the Qur'ān and other early classical texts. Here, too, Luṭfī does not grant religion in general, and Islam in particular, a central role in bringing about change. Luṭfī was far less inclined than Amīn to blame later Islam (or Christianity) for "backwardness" and "discrimination" against women. In his view, "general despotism" was responsible for the advancement and institutionalization of male chauvinist trends, thereby preventing women from achieving the freedom and equality they "naturally" deserved. Here, too, in other words, just as Islam and other religions had not caused the "backwardness" of the past, they had no role to play in bringing about progressive change in women's status in the present and future.[45]

---

**44** See, e.g., "al-Ḥurriyya [1]" (May 1912); "Ḥurriyyat al-Ra'y" (1912); "al-Ḥurriyya [3]" (December 1912); and see the series of articles published between December 18, 1913, and January 1, 1914: "Ḥurriyyatunā," "al-Ḥurriyya wa Madhāhib al-Ḥukm," "Ḥurriyyat al-Ta'līm," "Ḥurriyyat al-Qaḍā'," "Ḥurriyyat al-Ṣiḥāfa," "Ḥurriyyat al-Khiṭāba," Ḥurriyyat al-Ijtimā'," "Madhhab al-Ḥurriyya" and, finally, "Khātima," *MN*, II:60–67, 75–98.

**45** See Luṭfī al-Sayyid's early obituary for Qāsim Amīn, "Qāsim Amīn: al-Qudwa al-Ḥasana" (1908), *MN*, I:1–11; and see "Muḥarrir al-Mar'a" (1908), *MB*:148–159; "Banātunā wa Abnā'unā" (1908), *MN*, I:16–19; "Banātunā" (1909), *MN*, I:114–116; and "Al-Ḥaraka al-Nisā'iyya fī Miṣr" (1912), *MN*, I:268–271. See also *QH*:99–102.

## God in a New Role: Legitimizing Enlightenment, Modernity and Nationalism

What, then, is the role of religion in the new national reality? How does religion sit with the "Age of Enlightenment" and the present-day concepts of "modernity," "progress" and "freedom"? As noted, Luṭfī never considered himself a "secularist," and he was certainly not an atheist. At times he seemed to adopt secular ideas, norms and values, but, although the terms "secular" and "secularism" (*ʿilmānī, ʿilmāniyya*) existed in the Arabic political lexicon and public discourse, he avoided acknowledging them or using them himself. He seldom mentioned the *sharīʿa*, vehemently opposed religious orthodoxy and disregarded the *ʿulamāʾ* and their pretentions to serve as the exclusive interpreters of Islam and *sharīʿa*, but God nevertheless continued to be present in Luṭfī's writings and speeches. He never cast doubt on or hesitated about His presence. Luṭfī's God existed in both the personal and the collective spheres. In this respect, he rejected the secular "privatization of religion" that, by reducing religion to a private, personal matter between man and his God, removes God from the collective life.

A good starting point for understanding Luṭfī al-Sayyid's views on religion in the age of Enlightenment and nationalism may be found in a description by Albert Hourani of the socio-economic class in which Luṭfī was raised, the *ʿumda/ʿumad* stratum. Hourani rightly pointed out that this stratum was "the creative class of modern Egypt: the village families of some local standing with a tradition of learning and piety."[46] Notwithstanding the generational differences between him and his father, Luṭfī remained faithful to some kind of divine presence even in the modern state of Enlightenment, characterized as it was by freedom, progress and "the new woman." As we have seen, Luṭfī shed many of the values and norms of this rural social class, but he retained the belief that modernity does not "assassinate" God as a supreme being above and beyond all limiting boundaries of rational human reality.[47] Indeed, Luṭfī was in the habit of reminding readers of God in a variety of contexts, thus positioning himself as an opponent of the atheist secularism professed by some of the great European Enlightenment thinkers. To be sure, he felt an affinity with those thinkers who saw a contradiction between Enlightenment, science and rationality, and continued faith in God. In their wake, Luṭfī attacked religious establishments and "organized religion," and he lambasted rituals and customs of traditional popular religion as "superstitions." However, thinkers like Locke, Montesquieu and Rousseau had

46 Hourani 1962:130.
47 *QH*:18–39, 69–77, 121–130.

sought a new type of religious belief that would maintain a role for God and divine providence in the modern world while avoiding religious fanaticism and encouraging tolerance and reconciliation between religions. Most of them, as Amos Hofman has said, "were men of faith. Even though they consistently and bitterly attacked the religious establishments, very few of them were professed atheists."[48] Luṭfī rejected, if not always directly, the secular atheist views developed by other Enlightenment thinkers such as Diderot, Holbach and Helvetius,[49] and he never shared their doubts about divine revelation, prophets or the presence of God in the world.

Luṭfī was well acquainted with Voltaire and admired his position as a public intellectual who constantly and fearlessly goaded political and religious establishments. But Luṭfī never fully accepted the French philosopher's crushing attacks on the essence of religion and God.[50] Hence, contrary to a commonly held scholarly claim that Luṭfī, in a simplistic imitation of European historical patterns, clung to the "desire of separating church and state,"[51] he never actually advocated a formal separation of religion and state. There is no mention in his writings of the struggle of the French Revolution against the monarchy and the church, and for the separation of religion from state. This approach was not only a product of Luṭfī's realistic understanding of the nature of the Egyptian community, most if not all of whose members, whether Muslims, Coptic Christians or Jews, preserved their religious traditions in different ways, so that, as a public intellectual, he had to consider how to reach out and appeal to these religious audiences. It also ensued from his enlightened religious observance and his worldview, and from the place in which he was born and raised. Luṭfī did not see modern life without the presence of God as granting legitimacy to the type of Enlightenment that celebrates religious tolerance and multi-vocal pluralism, freedom of religious choice and religious belief, without forcing religion onto political or national life. He sought ways to reintegrate religion, or rather, religions, into the concept of a modern revolutionary reality based on science, rationalism and social progress.[52] This approach, again, was inspired by a number of Enlightenment philosophers, particularly Immanuel Kant, as we shall see.

It is clear, then, that Luṭfī's modernist religiosity was not associated with the Islamic reformist agenda of Muḥammad ʿAbduh, which uses *ijtihād* to reinterpret

**48** Hofman 2012:138.

**49** *Ibid.*:138–149; see also Pagden 2013:96–242.

**50** "Al-Inklīz fī Miṣr aw Intiqād Kitāb *Miṣr al-Ḥadītha*, Taʾlīf al-Lūrd Krūmar" (1908), *SM*:106–112.

**51** Wendell 1972:229.

**52** "Ilā al-shabība" (1910), *MN*, I:183–185.

and redefine classical texts in order to prove their relevance to modern reality. This "game" with the Islamic past, ancient or classical, appeared artificial and unproductive to Luṭfī. He also rejected the formation of a modern system of government ruled by an Islamic "benevolent despot" (*al-mustabidd al-ādil*), an idea attributed to ʿAbduh, who considered it "the ideal government" for the modern Muslim community. Luṭfī saw in this model a false utopian regime. There cannot be an "absolutist regime based on foundations of justice," he argued; "this is a fantastical/imagined theory of a [political] regime that history has never known." Even if, "in the beginning of Islam," in the era of the "rightly guided caliphs" (*al-khulafāʾ al-rāshidūn*), "an autocratic regime was both conditional and restrained, in that its official conduct was subject, in all its social and political activities, to Allah's Qurʾān and the Sunna of the Prophet ... and therefore it did not violate the rights of the [Islamic] *umma*," declared Luṭfī, "the parliamentary representative government" was clearly "better and more suitable," and, in fact, "the human experience has proven that it is the best of all forms of government." In order to realize freedom in the age of Enlightenment, he wrote, "we must break the regime of absolutism and transition into a parliamentary representative government that is the government of the nation."[53] Moreover, in stark contrast to ʿAbduh, who places the blame for tyranny and the disruption of Islam solely on Turkish elements, and specifically on the post-ʿAbbasid eras of the Mamluks and the Ottomans, Luṭfī claims that, with the exception of the short period of the *rāshidūn* caliphs at the inception of Islam, every Islamic government and regime was an "unjust absolutist government."[54] The view held by many scholars that Luṭfī al-Sayyid may be considered an "adherent" or a "disciple" of Muḥammad ʿAbduh is thus misguided; in fact, ʿAbduh is rarely mentioned in Luṭfī's hundreds of articles. Luṭfī's religious modernity was decidedly different.[55]

In Luṭfī's terms, the location of religion in modern life demands, first and foremost, a new and precise definition of the location of Islam in the context of modernity. Just as he empties Islam of socio-political meaning, Luṭfī divests Islam of all its claims to superiority, chosenness, exceptionality and historical singularity. Luṭfī's Islam is not based in the *sharīʿa*. It is not the central player on the human stage, and its doctrine is not the highest, the last or the best of the religious doctrines – specifically in relation to Christianity and Judaism. Only social systems that encourage religious pluralism, multivocality and heterogeneity of belief held by faith communities unified under national hegemony are tenable

---

**53** "Ḥuqūq al-Umma" (1914), *TA*:101–104; see also "al-Ḥurriyya al-Shakhṣiyya" (1913), *TA*:87–94.
**54** "Ḥuqūq al-Umma" (1914) , *TA*:101–104; on this see also Wendell 1972:226–229.
**55** See, e.g., Hourani 1970:170–179; Ahmed 1960:35–112; Wendell 1972:185–293.

in the age of Enlightenment. In other words, Luṭfī's liberal nationalism dictated a liberal, pluralistic approach to Islam and to Egyptian Muslims. Luṭfī repeatedly and systematically rejected every "fanatical" element associated with Islam: militancy, aggression, intolerance for other religions and beliefs, and the religious persecution of non-Muslims. "A decent and honest man," he wrote, "cannot afford to allow religious fanaticism (*al-taʿaṣṣub al-dīnī*) to govern his existence."[56] The enlightened lover of freedom and progress contains his religion in a nationalist, multi-religious framework.

Islam, in Luṭfī's view, thus is not and cannot be "the nation of Muslims" or the "unified Islamic association," which he saw as encouraging religious fanaticism, aggression and hostility toward non-Islamic religions and beliefs. For Luṭfī, "the true Islamic faith is found solely in the commandments of cooperation, help, support and association between the individuals of the [Egyptian] nation; as it simultaneously commands justice, encourages good behavior and just relations with allies from other religious communities." Therefore, "the fundamentals of Islam do not at all recognize perverse fanaticism," which is entirely foreign to the true Islam.[57]

Among themselves, Muslims believe in "one religion" based on a "unity of faith" and the cultivation of "love and mutual support," practiced "in various forms and modes according to pluralistic understandings of the essence of religion." This "unity of faith" does not contradict the "multiple interpretations and understandings" of Islam carried out in accordance with a multiplicity of forms and practices in worship of the Creator. The will of the God of Islam is expressed in a variety of heterogeneous ideas, patterns and shades. Herein lies the "attraction" and "fascination" of Islam that one must ponder and act upon. This "apolitical and non-fanatical" Islam, which recognizes the supremacy of the nation and the right of individuals to live together in mutual cooperation with other beliefs and opinions, is the Islam that is suitable for modern life, the life of "freedom, civilization and progress."[58]

As noted above, Luṭfī was convinced that the ascription of "religious fanaticism" (*al-taʿaṣṣub al-dīnī*) to Egyptians, or to Muslims in general, originated in the colonialist perception. Like the "invention" of "pan-Islamic unity," the "fiction" of "Islamic extremism" was a colonial anti-Islamic construct. Here, too, the British rule in Egypt, particularly since Eldon Gorst had begun his term as Consul General (1907), played an active role in creating the image of violent and fanatical

---

**56** "Taqrīr al-Lūrd Krūmar: al-Taʿaṣṣub al-dīnī" (1907), *SM*:102.
**57** *Ibid.*
**58** *Ibid.*, *SM*:102–105.

Egyptian Muslims. With studied politeness and restraint, Luṭfī repeatedly exposes the colonial hostility and malevolence behind these images of Muslims as "evil fanatics." The intentions of European (British) colonialism are clear to him: The representation of Egyptians as "religious fanatics" was aimed at fueling hatred and hostility against them, proving their backwardness and primitiveness, and legitimizing the continuation of colonial occupation, exploitation, oppression and suppression. According to the colonizers, the Muslims deserved to be colonized "because they are Muslims," and the Europeans were meant to be colonizers "because they are Christians." To Luṭfī's mind, adopting this colonialist, racist Orientalism, and turning Muslims and Arabs into "religious fanatics," permitted the colonizers to persecute Muslims, despise their faith, and ridicule and humiliate Islam. Exploiting the power of the occupation, they sought to demonstrate the inferiority, backwardness and impotence of Islam, while preventing Muslims from internalizing the values of the Enlightenment and modernity.

Even worse, according to Luṭfī, the colonial rule was not ready to accept that Egyptians were also striving for Enlightenment, intellectual progress, freedom and modern education. The colonialists knew that "also in our [Egyptian] current situation, we need to borrow European modernity/civilization." The Egyptians justly sought to acquire competence and skills "to compete with everyone else [in Europe] with civilized and modern lives" and "to gain the necessary strength to cope with [modern] life." However, the imperial occupier was not ready to recognize that this desire for modernity, which included a willingness to accept Enlightenment values and practices from Europe, came from Egyptian Muslims "in peaceful ways," with openness, moderation and tolerance.[59] Luṭfī blames "government officials and British colonial officers" for fostering

> the fault of religious fanatics ... in order to put a barrier between us and our inclination toward European liberals and to distance us from those [European] men of money and power who want to invest in Egyptian interests for the good of the Egyptian people.

This "prevents us from obtaining the economic aid and political support" that is essential for the development and prosperity of Egypt. It also distances "us" from other (European or Middle Eastern) political and financial powers that could "monitor the arbitrary activities [of the British] in Egypt."[60] No less seriously, the British colonialists blame Egyptians for Islamic fanaticism in order to prevent them from exercising "their natural right" to an independent government.

---

**59** "al-Taqlīd" (1913), *TA*:80–83; "Al-Ḥāla al-Ḥāḍira" (1908), *MB*:82–84; "Ḥadīth al-Sir Eldon Gorst" (1908), *SM*:155–160.

**60** "Al-Ḥāla al-Ḥāḍira" (1908), *MB*:76; "Taqrīr al-Lūrd Krūmar" (1907), *SM*:96–99.

Charges of "xenophobia against foreigners" and "Islamic fanaticism" are the "most effective weapon" of these colonialists "to convince their nation and the entire European world, and even, with a special effort, to convince us, the Egyptians, of the futility of our fight for self-government (*al-ḥukm al-dhātī*) that would lead Egypt to independence (*al-istiqlāl*)."[61]

Notwithstanding his carefully maintained restraint, Luṭfī's meaning is clear. The aim of colonialism is to "civilize" the Muslims, to remove the "fanaticism that they do not have" and eventually to eliminate their Islamic identity itself. Even when it occasionally realized that it could trust in the Egyptians and in their abilities to change and modernize, the colonial regime was afraid to acknowledge this, for then the colonizers would have to recognize "their original sin": the inherently belligerent nature and demonic, negative and imperialist character of colonialism. This would undermine colonialism's *raison d'être* and negate its perceived right to occupy and exploit other nations weaker than itself. Thus, Luṭfī charges, the white man's burden rests on the religious defamation of Muslims, for the sake of perpetuating and legitimizing the white man's rule over their "inferiors" and their "suppression" of the deplorable, primitive, "fanaticism" that they see as built into all Muslims and into Islam.[62]

This entire image is a forgery. Luṭfī defines this "pseudo-religious fanaticism" (*al-taʿaṣṣub al-dīnī al-mawhūm*) as a "vile/obscene accusation" (*al-tuhma al-shanīʿa*) against Egyptian Muslims.[63] He was convinced that, in the Egyptian reality, there was "no such thing" as intolerance, either by Muslims against Christians (and Jews) or by Muslims against other Muslims. Challenging the colonial stereotype, Luṭfī argues that any reference to religious fanaticism in Egypt is "unfounded and completely false .... It has no basis in religion and no foundation in the hearts of Muslims." Those who hurled the accusation of "Islamic fanaticism, or pan-Islamism against us, the Egyptians, ... know themselves, as we know, that the Egyptians are the people farthest from this [contemptible] fault and are surely the most innocent."[64] Christian Europe might boast of Enlightenment, humanism, progress, religious and racial tolerance and moral superiority, but, for many long generations, it had fought religious wars and perpetrated religious

61 "Al-Ḥāla al-Ḥāḍira" (1908), *MB*:71–77; "Fī Sabīl al-Ḥukm al-Dhātī" (1907), *SM*:113–114; "Al-Ḥukm al-Dhātī: al-Taʿlīm al-ʿāmm," part 1 (1907), *SM*:115–117; "al-ʿĀm al-Thānī li-Siyāsat al-Wifāq" (1908), *SM*:153–154.

62 "Al-Ḥāla al-Ḥāḍira" (1908), *MB*:64–91.

63 "Taqrīr al-Lūrd Krūmar: al-Taʿaṣṣub al-dīnī" (1907), *SM*:103.

64 *Ibid.*, *SM*:103–105; "Al-Ḥāla al-Ḥāḍira" (1908), esp. *MB*:75–76.

persecution, to the point of massacring members of other religions. That violent history was now embodied in the European imperialist project.

In stark contrast to Europe, Egyptian society demonstrates "that Copts can live with Muslims, mixing interests and shared lives, living in shared homes and neighborhoods, working shoulder to shoulder in rural agriculture and other jobs, sitting as neighbors side by side at school desks [and] as colleagues in positions as government officials, sharing public resources channeled toward the public good."[65] Luṭfī's Egypt is a paragon of harmony, shared lives and tolerance between different religions. Europe and its colonialists ought to learn this lesson from Egypt, rather than turning it into a pawn for the perpetuation of illegitimate imperialist exploitation.[66] For some time, as Luṭfī emphasized:

> We have not heard that the Muslims in Egypt, who were commanded by their religion to perform only good deeds, fomented hostility or aggression, nor have they erupted against their brothers [from other religions] or acted as though religious fanaticism had awoken hatred and animosity in their souls, causing them to raise up their arms intentionally to harm the [country's] shared interests and benefits.[67]

In the modern era, Luṭfī concludes, it is the framework of national identity, and not that of religious identity, that defines the Egyptian, Muslim, Copt or Jew.[68] Egyptians have one national voice and many religious voices; there is a united Egyptian national fraternity, open inclusively to the existence of different beliefs, religions and gods.

Luṭfī sees no contradiction between nationalism and God. On the contrary, to his mind, loyalty to a single national collective and a single homeland is natural, a product of "the creation" or "the natural order of things" (*al-fiṭra*). God's working attests to and solidifies this "human nature." He understands the "natural" and "utilitarian" human need to adhere to a nation and a homeland, to love them and to devote oneself to them. Indeed, He has "armed all His creatures with the weapon of defending their [national] identity" and insisted on their right to independence and sovereignty.[69] Naturally, says Luṭfī,

---

**65** "Taqrīr al-Lūrd Krūmar: al-Taʿaṣṣub al-dīnī" (1907), *SM*:102–103.

**66** *Ibid.*, *SM*:102–105.

**67** *Ibid.*, *SM*:102–103. Obviously, Luṭfī al-Sayyid couldn't have anticipated that three years later, in 1910, Butrus Ghali, the Coptic Prime Minister, would be assassinated by an active member of the Nationalist Party, a Muslim by the name of Ibrāhīm Nāṣif al-Wardānī.

**68** Public address in Alexandria (1908), *SM*:33–34; "Naḥnu wa al-Istiqlāl" (1908), *SM*:126–129; "Taqrīr al-Lūrd Krūmar: al-Taʿaṣṣub al-dīnī" (1907), *SM*:102–105; see also *QH*:73–77.

**69** "Al-Ḥāla al-Ḥāḍira" (1908), *MB*:82–87; "Fa-'l-Nafham al-Istiqlāl" (1912), esp. *MB*:123–127; "Ilā al-shabība: al-iḍṭirāb fī al-ra'y al-ʿāmm" (1912), *MN*, I:307–312, *MB*:106–112.

> the Egyptian wants to live a national life (*ʿīsha qawmiyya*). Therefore, he is striving to achieve political freedom, the inalienable right that God gave to His [national] collective from the day that this collective community settled in their defined homeland (territory).[70]

But Luṭfī was not satisfied with the definition of a new place for Islam in the context of a liberal national modernity. As someone who also believed in a universal transnational society of multi-religious tolerance, he sought to formulate a more general attitude toward religion and divinity. Luṭfī believed almost axiomatically that "divine providence" had inspired the modern Enlightenment project. This divine providence was not necessarily Islamic. God attested and effectuated His Enlightenment project, and its translation to the Egyptian reality was not only possible but also necessary. Given that the adaptation of *tamaddun* to the Egyptian environment was also a question of survival, God recognized its necessity, stood behind it and blessed it. Similarly, "God rejects all religious fanaticism," and "religion (Islam, but also Christianity and Judaism) is much more tolerant than people think and consider it to be."[71] More specifically, in all dimensions of modern enlightened life, God stands as caretaker, protector and provider of sympathy and consent, and acts as judge. He expresses His disapproval of all religious chauvinism, ethnocentrism, exclusivity and supremacy, and of discrimination and persecution on the basis of religion. Luṭfī's God is not only consistent with modernity; He also endows it with His spirit and powers, lending it legitimacy. Therefore, according to Luṭfī, "the nature of human civilization" (*ṭabīʿat al-tamaddun al-insānī*) does not require sophisticated, scientific or philosophical justification; it is "something known and accepted," also by the holy *sharīʿa*, as the word of God and the fulfillment of His wishes.[72]

Sometimes, in a more apologetic and rhetorical way, Luṭfī interprets the essence of the divine revelation to the Prophet and the creation of the first community of believers as an early Enlightenment expression. God's Prophet Muḥammad and his disciples, he wrote, "came into the world to purify the universe of the abomination and filth of the ancient *jāhiliyya*; in order to establish on its ruins a strong civilization founded on the basis of purification of the heart and release from the shackles of the old vanity and impurity."[73] In other words, the Enlightenment era, which Luṭfī experienced with great intensity, could have also been inspired by the revelation to the Prophet Muḥammad and the creation of Islam.

---

**70** "Ilā al-shabība: Gharaḍ al-Umma huwa al-Istiqlāl" (1912), esp. *MN*, I:315.

**71** Public address in Alexandria (1908), *SM*:34, 36; "Muḥarrir al-Mar'a" (1908), *MB*:153.

**72** "Al-Ḥāla al-Ḥāḍira" (1908), *MB*:82–83.

**73** "Awwal al-ʿĀm" (1911), *MN*, I:257–258.

In this spirit, Luṭfī can say that freedom is born of the "natural human condition" and that God knows this freedom and "delegates authority to it." As he wrote, "God created them [human beings] as people of freedom, free to say and to write what they wish, free to do what they please";[74] "The laws of nature ... give every person/individual the right to freedom, because God did not create man to be feeble and poor [deprived of liberty]."[75] Luṭfī also invokes Divine inspiration in his constant struggle against "absolute tyranny." He is convinced that his systematic exhortations, in dozens of articles, for constitution, parliament and democracy rest in God's command: God "is the witness that personal [autocratic] rule has no right to survive in this [modern] era."[76]

Luṭfī advocates the removal of religion as a basis for the conduct of political life, which should be based exclusively on "interests and benefits ... [and the] transition to utility as the sole basis for politics and political action." For him, this utilitarian perception is consistent with "the true religion" (*al-dīn al-ḥanīf*, monotheism, Islam).[77] Even the new politics, transpiring in the open public sphere and influenced by "public opinion" (*al-ra'y al-ʿāmm*), receives the approval of God. Luṭfī believed that both "the shaping of political consciousness" and "the necessity of political participation" by all sons and daughters of the Egyptian nation were required to change "our terrible political situation" of occupation, lack of economic and political independence, autocratic Khedivial government, and clumsy, corrupt and inefficient bureaucracy. "Bringing about political progress" for the country was both a "collective duty" (*farḍ kifāya*) and a "personal duty" (*farḍ ʿayn*), "imposed on all of us."[78]

Changing the status of Muslim women and furthering their rights to emancipation from the shackles of male chauvinist political despotism and religious orthodoxy were also consistent with the divine will. According to Luṭfī, God knows "the nature" of the freedom of women, and that they deserve equality, modernity and Enlightenment: "The woman was created by nature as a free agent. Allah gave her freedom and sanctified it."[79] Equality of men and women and equal rights for different classes and groups within the nation must ensue both from the provisions and practices of the Islamic *sharīʿa* (*al-sharīʿa al-islāmiyya*) and from the

**74** "al-Ḥurriyya [2]" (September 1912), esp. *MB*:132–133.

**75** Public address (1909), *SM*:44.

**76** "Anṣār Sulṭatayn" (1908), esp. *SM*:151; "Khātima" (1914), esp. *MN*, II:96.

**77** "Ilā al-shabība: al-iḍṭirāb fī al-Ra'y al-ʿāmm" (1912), *MN*, I:307–312, *MB*:109–110.

**78** "Al-Ḥāla al-Ḥāḍira" (1908), *MB*:82–83.

**79** "Taʿlīm al-Mar'a Asās al-Iṣlāḥ al-Ijtimāʿi" (1908), esp. *MB*:172–173; "Lā Tuḍāyyiqū ʿAlayhinna?" (1908), esp. *MN*, I:35; *QH*:99–102.

modern concepts and practices of western civilization (*al-tamaddun al-gharbī*)."[80] Luṭfī went so far as to claim that "divine protection" and "the blessing of God" pertained to the reformist philosophy of Qāsim Amīn, Egypt's "liberator of women." Luṭfī, who admired Amīn and dedicated a series of articles to him, believed that he was "a masterpiece of Allah," "an extraordinary talent," whom God gave "integrity" and "excellence"; he was a prime example of a pioneering intellectual leader, who had brought the doctrine of "the new woman" to the Egyptian nation and other nations in the Islamic Arab world. Amīn's teachings about the freedom of women, their independence, respecting their right to education and employment, removal of the veil, liberation from seclusion, and the right to leave even a monogamous marriage were supported and incentivized by God.[81]

Modern conduct also requires ethical behavior and moral virtues. Luṭfī, himself a moralist, wrote extensively about moral issues and was the first to translate Aristotle's *Nicomachean Ethics* into Arabic.[82] He saw in religion the foundation of a solid system of modern ethical values and norms. True, the modern era had created a revolution in human life and society; yet, despite the sanctification of reason and science, man could not create a totally new ethical philosophy that was entirely independent of norms and values developed in the pre-modern era. For Luṭfī, Aristotle's *Ethics*, along with the ethical concepts of Enlightenment writers, corresponded with the ethics of the monotheistic religions. Together they created a foundation for moral thought and behavior in the modern age. In his articles, Luṭfī dedicated considerable space to the topics of personal and public morality: good and evil, justice and injustice, happiness and sadness, beauty and ugliness, loyalty and betrayal, friendship and hatred, honesty and hypocrisy, happiness and misery, wealth and poverty, humility and arrogance, negligence against accountability, and even life and suicide. He saw in the Enlightenment a new surrounding in which man and society could perfect and better themselves and their moral behavior in all these areas and, in so doing, rise to unprecedented virtue. In this context he turned to Aristotle and to the writings of Enlightenment philosophers, but also always to the divine presence of God and to the ethical concepts developed in monotheistic Islamic and non-Islamic cultures. When it came to Egypt, Luṭfī explained,

---

**80** "Muḥarrir al-Mar'a" (1908), esp. *MB*:153–156; *QH*:99–102.

**81** "Muḥarrir al-Mar'a" (1908), *MB*:148–149; "Qāsim Amīn: al-Qudwa al-Ḥasana" (1908), *MN*, I:1–11; "Tarbiyat al-Banāt" (1911), *MN*, I:226–228.

**82** Luṭfī al-Sayyid's full translation of Aristotle's *Nicomachean Ethics* into Arabic was first published in Cairo in 1924.

> the principle of good and evil draws from a belief in the foundations of religion ... from the ethical concept that religion is the basis of general education and morality. There is no doubt that all the divine faiths (Islam, Judaism and Christianity) command one to do good and prohibit bad deeds. [On an ethical level] they all preach faith in God and in the world to come."[83]

For example, Luṭfī claims that "the right [of a man] to divorce is not to be taken for granted unless there are serious reasons"; that is, the woman's position and her rights are to be taken fully into account before her husband can divorce her. "Otherwise," he warns, the divorce will be an arbitrary act "of hostility and oppression, and God forbade acts of injustice and ordered Muslims to remove injustice." Beyond supporting the ideas of Qāsim Amīn, Luṭfī states here that "arbitrary" actions, oppression, evil and injustice are abominations, forbidden by divine authority to both Muslims and non-Muslims.[84]

In formulating his agenda concerning proper education in the modern state, Luṭfī demanded: "Religion [all religions] must remain one of the foundations of moral education so that the [educated] Egyptian will not lose his character and substance."[85] More generally, in speaking of the prescribed ethical norms by which an individual must behave in his home and in the public sphere, Luṭfī refers constantly to Aristotle's *Ethics* and simultaneously to the divine religious ethics of Islam, but also of Judaism and Christianity. In Luṭfī's approach to religion as a moral source, we also see the impact of Immanuel Kant, in particular his late writings, such as *Die Religion innerhalb der Grenzen der bloßen Vernunft* (Religion within the limits of reason alone, 1793). Luṭfī adopted Kant's assumption that morality, by its very nature, requires a direct connection to God: "Morality thus leads ineluctably to religion, through which it extends itself to the idea of a powerful moral Lawgiver, outside of humankind," that is, in the divine. Religion provides the highest standard of moral perfection to which man and society aspire; it is indispensable for the modern man as a complement to his national, rational life.[86] Religion ensures the will to aim for ultimate perfection and attempt to realize it in one's lifetime. Luṭfī, following Kant, was convinced that the modern

**83** "Al-Ḥukm al-Dhātī: al-Taʿlīm al-ʿāmm," part 2 (1907), *SM*:118–119; "Fī al-Akhlāq: al-Riyāʾ" (1908), *MN*, I:49–52. For this point, see also Hourani 1970:172–173.

**84** "Banātunā wa Abnāʾunā [2]" (1913), esp. *MN*, II:154. See also "Fī al-Akhlāq: al-Bighāʾ" (1911), *MN*, I:262–265.

**85** "Ilā al-shabība: Wasāʾil al-Istiqlāl, al-Tarbiya wa-al-Taʿlīm" (1912), esp. *MN*, I:330; "al-Tarbiya wa-al-Taʿalīm" (1912), esp. *MN*, II:9; "Al-Ḥukm al-Dhātī: al-Taʿlīm al-ʿāmm," part 2 (1907), *SM*:119–120.

**86** Kant 1793, 1960: Introduction to the first German edition.

enlightened and civilized man required religion to guide him and supervise his moral behavior.

## Conclusion: Toward Modern Religious Pluralism

Aḥmad Luṭfī al-Sayyid's endeavor to create a local Egyptian Enlightenment "able to compete with modern nations and cultures" did not place religion at the center of the transition into modernity that Egypt was then experiencing. Luṭfī was a rationalist, a humanist and a liberal: Human beings, their free will, their reason and especially their interests and utilities, and their freedom to define and understand them, were the keys to progress toward self and collective refinement and civilization (*tamaddun*). According to Luṭfī, in the modern era of freedom, progress and rationality, of science and utilitarianism, advancing and actualizing these elements are the actions of the free men and women – of those who choose to be "civilized" (*mutamaddin*) and, by the power of their will, have the liberty to do so.

True, modern man and society have "founding fathers": "the first and highest teacher," Aristotle, and to a lesser extent, for Muslims, the philosophers Al-Fārābī, Ibn Sīnā, Ibn Bāja and Ibn Rushd. Luṭfī was versed in and admired all of these philosophers and saw himself and his philosophy as an extension of their project. But only in the seventeenth, eighteenth and nineteenth centuries, were the noble ideas and values of the Enlightenment emancipated from the shackles of traditional orthodox religion and reactionary conservatism, and they thereby received new meanings and configurations. To a great extent, therefore, modernity was a new and unparalleled phenomenon in human history. The changes in the status of women and the vision of a free woman with equal rights to that of men was, for Luṭfī, among the unique, unprecedented features of modernity.

In this sense, Luṭfī was an essentialist modernist in his belief that he was sharing in the supreme human experience, more progressive and perfect than all of its historical predecessors. He somewhat naively believed that modernity, for the first time, held the true key to the emancipation of humanity and society, and it would bring them to lofty ideals and noble virtues. He saw his role as a public intellectual as one of inculcating the wider Egyptian public with the "modern consciousness": uprooting the old, lost, archaic traditional world and replacing it with the new, modern world of Enlightenment. However, for Luṭfī, though he distanced God from politics, society and culture, this unprecedented, innovative Enlightenment project did not eliminate God and religious sentiment from the modern human experience, to which His existence was still indispensable.

To be sure, traditional, totalitarian religious authority and orthodox monotheistic dogma had been upended by the Enlightenment. Man, not God, was master of his universe, determining the course of his own life, changing the present and framing the future. God remained essential, but in a different role. Luṭfī, more than any other Egyptian intellectual or philosopher inspired by the European Enlightenment, seems to have been impacted in this by Leo Tolstoy – his literary works, his values and moods and, in particular, his humanist worldview. Luṭfī admired the great Russian writer and studied his way of life and worldview with great interest.[87] Luṭfī and his contemporaries among Egypt's public intellectuals saw Tolstoy as a model. His unique social stratum of Russian intelligentsia was an educated and sophisticated, if somewhat narrow and limited elite, faced with hordes of illiterate peasants and the dilemma of how to integrate the Enlightenment and impart it to wider sectors of society; and it, too, was working from the periphery rather than from Western Europe. Luṭfī expressed his admiration for Tolstoy in several articles and dedicated an impressive and insightful eulogy to him in November 1910.[88]

Luṭfī saw Tolstoy, in his attitude toward religion, as a spiritual father and a partner in thought, feeling and faith. As Luṭfī aspired to be, Tolstoy was a nationalist with a universal and humanistic worldview:

> [F]irst and foremost he was a man who loved his nation, but who could find sympathy for its enemies ... not only a Russian man, but a man of the world and of peace. ... [He] was not a dogmatic Christian who limited his feelings and emotions within the boundaries of sacred texts or traditions of the orthodox Christian church. ... He was not a narrow-minded Christian, fanatical in his adherence to a particular Christian church. ... [He] was a Christian who fostered [religious] tolerance ... a tolerant man ready to adopt only noble religion, one that is not limited to any specific school of religion, but is open to the universal humane school of thought.

This was because:

> Tolstoy's heart was wide enough to accommodate a large quantity of the faithful of a particular religion, as well as those who disagreed with him [i.e., believers of other religions]. He saw in religion a pure source for the soul and the heart, for emotions, and a source of love for those who were close to him, and for the others who were distant. In his work he brought happiness into this world and even into the next.[89]

87 "al-Marʾa Ayḍan" (1908), *MN*, I:80–82.
88 "Māta al-Rajul" (1910), *MN*, I:192–196.
89 *Ibid.*, *MN*, I:193–194. See also "al-Istiqlāl al-Dhātī" (1911), *MN*, I:201–203; and *QH*:146–150.

For Luṭfī, similarly, religion could not be derived from the authority of Islamic law or orthodoxy. He was oblivious to the *'ulamā*, of whom there is hardly a mention in his many writings, and he also did not accept Muḥammad 'Abduh's Islamic modernist-reformist project. In Luṭfī's thought, the essentialism and uniqueness of Islam as the final and perfect religious monotheistic doctrine must be replaced with religious pluralism, tolerance for other religions and granting them equal status in the modern national community. In an era in which Egypt must first and foremost become a modern nation, religion (Islam, but also Christianity and Judaism) must mobilize to advance the objectives of that nation: liberation, progress, independence, sovereignty, advanced education, personal and collective freedom, the adoption of science and technology, the emancipation of women, the development of critical public opinion and a pluralist political culture, and establishing a constitutional parliamentary political system. All these modern norms, values, and practices, developed and refined under the influence of the Enlightenment, not only do not contradict religious norms and values; they can and must comply with them in a harmony of cooperative effort and mutual feedback. Modernity is possible only within the national framework, and religious faith has an essential role to play in it, in providing incentives and promoting the abilities and skills of the nation to internalize and domesticate the *tamaddun*, to become "a civilized nation."

These conclusions regarding Aḥmad Luṭfī al-Sayyid's relocation of religion in modern times fit well with the findings of other scholars who have highlighted the complex relationship between Islam and modernity, particularly under colonialism. Luṭfī and others dismantled the binary oppositions between religion and secularism, traditional religion and innovative modernity, science and religion, and state and religion. They rejected the simplistic notion that rationality, science, freedom, progress and equality[90] can develop only in a "post-traditional" age of "post-religious Enlightenment," that "the death of God" and the expurgation of religion from modern life are prerequisites for the very establishment of the modern Enlightenment. In fact, Luṭfī believed, religion remained essential in the complex reality of true modern Enlightenment, in both non-European and European societies and cultures. In this sense, the binaries of "West" and the "East" also fall apart in Luṭfī's philosophy.

Early in the twenty-first century, anthropologist Talal Asad argued that the categories of "religious" and "secular" are not rigid in nature, that "the sacred and the secular are dependent on one another,"[91] and so "religion is far from

**90** See, e.g., Dressler 2015.
**91** Asad 2003:39.

disappearing from the modern world" and in fact takes an active role in it.[92] These ideas are reflected in Luṭfī's much earlier writings, in which he follows Kant in situating the role of religion "within the borders of rationalism alone."[93] That role must be defined by clear-cut criteria of a liberal, progressive, pluralistic nationalism that allowed for multiple religions, religious tolerance and multi-vocal religious observance. In promoting the objectives and norms of liberal nationalism, Luṭfī strove to show that religion, after assuming a new meaning and form, can and should exist in the age of post-religious Enlightenment as well. Man, as an individual and a national-social creature, is fulfilled as a modern and enlightened being only if God is involved in the realization of this process, by guiding it and complementing its rationalism and its freedom, and by endowing it with legitimacy and moral standards.

## References

Writings by Aḥmad Luṭfī al-Sayyid

*JA* = *Al-Jarīda*, daily newspaper edited by Luṭfī al-Sayyid.
*MB* = *Mabādiʾ fī al-Siyāsa wa al-Adab wa al-Ijtimāʿ*. Cairo 1963.
*MN* = *al-Muntakhabāt*, ed. Ismāʿīl Maẓhar, I–II. Cairo 1937–1945.
*QH* = *Qiṣṣat Ḥayātī*. Cairo 1962.
*SM* = *Ṣafaḥāt Matwiyya*, ed. Ismāʿīl Maẓhar. Cairo 1946.
*TA* = *Taʾammulāt fī al-Falsafa wa al-Adab wa al-Siyāsa wa al-Ijtimāʿ*[2], ed. Ismāʿīl Maẓhar. Cairo 1946.

"al-ʿĀm al-Thānī li-Siyāsat al-Wifāq," *JA*, October 15, 1908; *SM*:153–154.
"Aʿmālunā," *JA*, March 2, 1913; *MB*:217–221.
"ʿAlaykum Anfusakum," *JA*, September 7, 1909; *MN*, I:164–166.
"Anṣār al-Sulṭatayn," *JA*, September 6, 1908; *SM*:151–152.
"Awwal al-ʿĀm," *JA*, December 21, 1911; *MN*, I:257–258.
"Banātunā," *JA*, March 14, 1909; *MN*, I:114–116.
"Banātunā wa Abnāʾunā [1]" *JA*, June 11, 1908; *MN*, I:16–19.
"Banātunā wa Abnāʾunā [2]" *JA*, January 12, 1913; *MN*, II:154–158.
"Fa-'l-Nafham al-Istiqlāl," *JA*, September 2, 1912; *MB*:123–129.
"Fī al-Akhlāq: al-Bighāʾ," *JA*, December 30, 1911; *MN*, I:262–265.
"Fī al-Akhlāq: al-Riyāʾ," *JA*, November 1, 1908; *MN*, I:49–52.
"Fī Sabīl al-Ḥukm al-Dhātī," *JA*, September 15, 1907; *SM*:113–114 .
"Ḥadīth al-Sir Eldon Gorst," *JA*, October 29, 1908; *SM*:155–160.
"Al-Ḥāla al-Ḥāḍira," public address at the club of Ḥizb al-Umma, *JA*, May 17, 1908; *MB*:64–91.
"Al-Ḥaraka al-Nisāʾiyya fī Miṣr," *JA*, January 27, 1912; *MN*, I:268–271.

92 *Ibid.*:11, 277.
93 Kant 1793, 1960: Introductions to the first and second editions.

"Al-Ḥukm al-Dhātī: al-Taʿlīm al-ʿĀmm," parts 1–2, *JA*, September 16–17, 1907; *SM*:115–117 and 118–120.
"Ḥuqūq al-Umma," *JA*, January 10, 1914; *TA*:101–104.
"al-Ḥurriyya [1]," *JA*, May 1, 1912; *MN*, I:296–298.
"al-Ḥurriyya [2]," *JA*, September 19, 1912; *MB*:132–137.
"al-Ḥurriyya [3]," *JA*, December 12, 1912; *TA*:59–64.
"al-Ḥurriyya wa Madhāhib al-Ḥukm," *JA*, December 20, 2013; *MN*, II:64–67.
"al-Ḥurriyya al-Shakhṣiyya," *JA*, September 28, 1913; *TA*:87–94.
"Ḥurriyyat al-Ijtimāʿ," *JA*, December 29, 1913; *MN*, II:88–90.
"Ḥurriyyat al-Khiṭāba," *JA*, December 28, 1913; *MN*, II:86–87.
"Ḥurriyyat al-Qaḍāʾ," *JA*, December 25, 1913; *MN*, II:80–82.
"Ḥurriyyat al-Raʾy," *JA*, May 16, 1912; *MN*, I:299–302.
"Ḥurriyyat al-Ṣiḥāfa," *JA*, December 27, 1913; *MN*, II:83–85.
"Ḥurriyyat al-Taʿlīm," *JA*, December 24, 1913; *MN*, II:75–79.
"Ḥurriyyatunā," *JA*, December 18, 1913; *MN*, II:60–63.
"Ilā al-shabība," *JA*, January 13, 1910; *MN*, I:183–185.
"Ilā al-shabība: Gharaḍ al-Umma huwa al-Istiqlāl," *JA*, September 2, 1912; *MN*, I:313–318.
"Ilā al-shabība: al-iḍṭirāb fī al-raʾy al-ʿāmm," *JA*, September 1, 1912; *MN*, I:307–312; *MB*:106–112.
"Ilā al-shabība: Wasāʾil al-Istiqlāl, al-Tarbiya wa-al-Taʿlīm," *JA*, September 5, 1912; *MN*, I:327–332.
"Al-Inklīz fī Miṣr aw Intiqād Kitāb *Miṣr al-Ḥadītha*, Taʾlīf al-Lūrd Krūmar," *JA*, April 14, 1908; *SM*:106–112.
"al-Istiqlāl al-Dhātī," *JA*, January 30, 1911; *MN*, I:201–203.
"al-Jāmiʿa al-Miṣriyya [1]," *JA*, October 5, 1909; *MN*, I:170–172.
"al-Jāmiʿa al-Miṣriyya [2]," *JA*, October 9, 1909; *MN*, I:183.
"al-Khadīw," *JA*, March 31, 1907; *SM*:57–68.
"Khātima," *JA*, January 1, 1914; *MN*, II:95–98.
"Lā Tuḍāyyiqū ʿAlayhinna," *JA*, July 13, 1908; *MN*, I:33–36.
"al-Lūrd al-Krūmar Imām al-Taʾrīkh," *JA*, April 13, 1907; *SM*:69–74 (partial English translation: Wendell 1972:295–301).
"Madhhab al-Ḥurriyya," *JA*, December 31, 1913; *MN*, II:91–94.
"al-Marʾa Ayḍan," *JA*, November 26, 1908; *MN*, I:80–82.
"Māta al-Rajul," *JA*, November 24, 1910; *MN*, I:192–196.
"Miṣriyyatunā," *JA*, January 6, 1913; *TA*:69–71.
"al-Miṣriyya," *JA*, January 16, 1913; *TA*:72–74.
"Muḥarrir al-Marʾa," *JA*, April 25, 1908; *MB*:148–159.
"Naḥnu wa al-Istiqlāl," *JA*, April 8, 1908; *SM*:121–129.
Public address, *JA*, January 2, 1909; *SM*:39–56.
Public address in Alexandria, *JA*, August 23, 1908; *SM*:7–38.
"Qāsim Amīn: al-Qudwa al-Ḥasana," parts 1–2, *JA*, April 25–26, 1908; *MN*, I:1–6 and 7–11.
"al-Raʾy al-ʿāmm," *JA*, July 11, 1908; *MN*, I:28–32.
"al-Siyāsa al-Inklīziyya," *JA*, April 6, 1907; *SM*:75–76.
"Siyāsat al-Wifāq," *JA*, July 2, 1908; *SM*:137–139.
"Taʿlīm al-Marʾa Asās al-Iṣlāḥ al-Ijtimāʿi," *JA*, July 13, 1908; *MB*:169–173.
"Taḍāmununā," *JA*, January 2, 1913; *TA*:65–68.
"al-Taqlīd," *JA*, March 4, 1913; *TA*:80–83.
"Taqrīr al-Lūrd Krūmar," *JA*, May 7, 1907, *SM*:96–101.
"Taqrīr al-Lūrd Krūmar: al-Taʿaṣṣub al-dīnī," *JA*, May 8, 1907, *SM*:102–105.

"Tarbiyat al-Banāt," *JA*, June 6, 1911; *MN*, I:226–228.
al-Tarbiya wa-al-Taʿlīm," *JA*, September 28, 1912; *MN*, II:8–9.
"al-Umma wa-al-Ḥukūma," *JA*, March 23, 24 and 30, 1907; April 2, 3 and 6, 1907; and September 2, 1908; *MB*:28–62.
"Usbūʿ fī al-Madīna al-Munawwara," Parts 1–6, *JA*, August 10, 26, 27, 28, 29 and 30, 1911; *MN*, I:229–251.

Other Publications

Ahmed, J.M. 1960. *The Intellectual Origins of Egyptian Nationalism*. Oxford.
Aristotle. 1946. *al-Siyāsa* (Arabic transl. by Aḥmad Luṭfī al-Sayyid). Cairo.
Asad, Talal. 2003. *Formations of the Secular: Christianity, Islam, Modernity*. Stanford.
Dressler, Markus. 2015. "Rereading Ziya Gökalp: Secularism and the Reform of the Islamic State." *International Journal of Middle East Studies*, 47:511–531.
Goldschmidt, Arthur. 1968. "The Egyptian Nationalist Party, 1892–1919." In: P.M. Holt (ed.), *Political and Social Change in Modern Egypt*, London. 308–333.
Ḥamza, ʿAbd al-Laṭīf. 1958–1963 [1950–1956]. *Adab al-Maqāla al-Ṣuḥufiyya fī Miṣr*², I–VIII. Cairo. Reprinted 1995.
Hofman, Amos. 2012. *A Revolution of the Mind: Enlightenment and Revolution in Eighteenth-Century France* (Hebrew). Tel Aviv.
Hourani, Albert. 1970 [1962]. *Arabic Thought in the Liberal Age, 1798–1939*. London: Oxford University Press.
Kant, Immanuel. 1793. *Die Religion innerhalb der Grenzen der bloßen Vernunft*. Leipzig.
Kant, Immanuel. 1960. *Religion Within the Limits of Reason Alone* (English transl. by Theodore M. Greene & Hoyt H. Hudson). New York.
Luṭfī al-Sayyid, Afaf. 1968. *Egypt and Cromer: A Study in Anglo-Egyptian Relations*. London.
Magee, Bryan. 1987. *The Great Philosophers: An Introduction to Western Philosophy*. London.
Montesquieu, Charles de Secondat. 1889. *The Spirit of the Laws*. Cambridge.
al-Najjār, Ḥusayn Fawzī. 1963. *Luṭfī al-Sayyid wa-al-Shakhṣiyya al-Miṣriyya*. Cairo.
al-Najjār, Ḥusayn Fawzī. 1965. *Aḥmad Luṭfī al-Sayyid – Ustādh al-Jīl*. Cairo.
Pagden, Anthony. 2013. *The Enlightenment and Why It Still Matters*. New York.
Sharaf, ʿAbd al-ʿAzīz. 2002. *Luṭfī al-Sayyid: Faylasūf Ayqaẓa Ummatan*. Cairo.
al- Shalaq, Aḥmad Zakariyā. 1979. *Ḥizb al-Umma wa-Dawruhu fī al-Siyāsa al-Miṣriyya*. Cairo.
Toledano, Ehud R. 2015. "Muhammad Farid: Between Nationalism and Egyptian-Ottoman Diaspora." In: Anthony Gorman and Sossie Kasbarian (eds.), *Diasporas of the Modern Middle East: Contextualizing Community*. Edinburgh. 70–102.
Wendell, Charles. 1972. *The Evolution of the Egyptian National Image: From its Origins to Ahmad Lutfi al-Sayyid*. Berkeley, CA.

Christoph Schmidt

# Socrates against Christ? A Theological Critique of Michel Foucault's Philosophy of Parrhesia

## Introduction

In his 1983 lecture on the "The Government of Self and Others," Michel Foucault offers a definition of philosophy, manifested in the Socratic spirit of an art of life:

> Philosophy thus defined as the free courage of telling the truth so as to take ascendancy over others and conduct them properly, even at the risk of death, is, I think, the daughter of *parrēsia*.[1]

According to Foucault, this configuration of Parrhesia, philosophy and a way of life developed historically, by way of its concrete relations to politics, rhetoric and

1 Foucault 2010:342. I shall refer here principally to Foucault's lectures on Parrhesia, namely, *The Hermeneutics of the Subject* (Foucault 2005) and *The Courage of Truth* (Foucault 2011). In *Fearless Speech* (Foucault 2001a), Foucault gave a short account of his project on Parrhesia, which developed out of his engagement with the history of sexuality, especially *The Care of the Self* (Foucault 1986), where, in the conclusion (*ibid.*:235–240), Foucault compares the philosophical and the Christian forms of care (later developed as a basic aspect of Parrhesia). On the special relationship between Foucault and Kierkegaard, see the remark of the editor, Frédéric Gros, in *Hermeneutics of the Subject*: "Foucault was a great reader of Kierkegaard, although he hardly ever mentions this author, who nonetheless had for him an importance as secret as it was decisive" (Foucault 2005:23, n. 46). In fact, Foucault mentions Kierkegaard once, in his essay "What Is an Author?": "It is not enough, however, to repeat the empty affirmation that the author has disappeared. For the same reason it is not enough to keep repeating [...] that God and man have died a common death. Instead we must locate the space left empty by the author's disappearance, follow the distribution of gaps and breaches, and watch for the openings this disappearance uncovers. [...] To say that X's real name is actually Jacques Durand instead of Pierre Dupont is not the same as saying that Stendhal's name was Henri Beyle. One could also question the meaning and functioning of propositions like [...] 'Victor Eremita, Climacus, Anticlimacus, Frater Taciturnus, Constantine Constantius, all of these are Kierkegaard.'" (Foucault 1998b:209–210) In fact, Foucault's whole project becomes manifest in these sentences, affirming the centrality of the death of God as the point of departure for his understanding of sovereign subjectivity as a permanent practice of aesthetic transgression. Parrhesia is but another way of exploring the space left empty, so that the aesthetic Kierkegaard is read as an author who has discovered this space – without referring to the theological foundation of this aesthetics! In fact, Foucault tries to rehabilitate theological Parrhesia from the point of view of the death of God.

https://doi.org/10.1515/9783110723984-007

pedagogy, into an art and "technology" of the care of the self, which is not only concerned with telling the truth to the other, but aims at a harmony between life and the truth of the self. This parrhesiastic life finds its ultimate expression in the existential-political state of exception in which the self is prepared to attest to its truth by its death. Parrhesia culminates – as becomes evident in the Socratic apology – in a drama of truth, a clash between the self and the ruling powers.

In his detailed reconstruction of the various forms of Parrhesia in ancient culture, Foucault often compares the Socratic with the Christian ways of life, in order to point to analogies, transformations, transitions, similarities and differences between them. The reader becomes witness to a subtle game of drawing limits, reorganizing those limits and transgressing them, in which the historian Foucault reveals ever-new aspects of the Socratic versus the Christian parrhesiastic ways of life, while avoiding any attempt at a definition of the essence of human life or of the subject.

While in the classical age these limits seem to move constantly and thus create different configurations of analogy, transition and difference between the Socratic and Christian ways of life, Foucault draws a clear boundary between antiquity and the modern age, from which, in his alternative conception of the history of philosophy, the Christian Parrhesia and way of life is firmly excluded.

Foucault mobilizes Descartes, Kant, Nietzsche and modern avant-garde artists as witnesses in constructing his alternative conception of this parrhesiastic history of philosophy, affirming his point of departure in Nietzsche's proclamation of the death of God, the end of metaphysics and the end of all limited forms and essences of the self rooted in a fixed knowledge. The idea of an aesthetics of existence, which Nietzsche himself drew from the event of the "Death of God," not only is re-projected onto the Greek past, but ultimately it signifies a clear departure from Christianity. As Foucault repeatedly declares, the end and overcoming of the Christian God opens a new horizon of possibilities and practices of "selving" and thus, at the same time, of the advent of another god or other gods,[2] who will correspond to the aesthetics of sovereign subjectivity and of modern avant-garde existence as a life of exception and transgression.[3] On the

2 "Rather than the death of God [...], what Nietzsche's thought heralds is the end of his murderer; it is the explosion of man's face in laughter, the return of the masks" (Foucault 1970:420). This explosion of man's identity into a plurality of masks is the moment of the return of the gods, who are the complement of this aesthetic revolution. "Is that not what Nietzsche was paving the way for when, in the interior space of his language, he killed man and God both at the same time, and thereby promised with the Return the multiple and re-illumined light of the gods?" (*ibid.*:334).

3 From the outset, Foucault's thinking is concerned with the practice of transgression, which replaces the defined nature of man in God's creation and the metaphysical or ethical order. See

basis of this modern theo-aesthetics, informed by Nietzsche and then Hölderlin, Christianity ultimately finds itself replaced by the other gods.

My immediate concern here will be with two significant omissions or empty discursive sights in Foucault's account of Parrhesia in antiquity and modernity, which I shall take as a point of departure for a theological reflection upon and critique of Foucault's theo-aesthetics.

(1) In his very last lecture, on "The Courage of Truth" (1984), Foucault for the first time turns from the Church Fathers directly to the New Testament itself. His concern, among others, is with the apostles John and Paul. But here we are in for a surprise: Foucault does not mention the Parrhesia par excellence, the messianic, Christological Parrhesia – the self-revelation of God as Son in the testimony of the divine truth and the death on the cross.

Intentionally or not, what Foucault leaves out here is nothing less than the Christian parallel and counterpoint to the Socratic drama of parrhesiastic truth – the condition of the possibility of all Christian forms of Parrhesia. Adopting a concept from the great Catholic theologian Hans Urs von Balthasar, I call this event the "theo-drama" of Truth.[4]

This event is not omitted merely out of a kind of philological failure or accidental forgetfulness, since with it the immanent economy of the discourse on Parrhesia, and its historical framework, would suffer an "interruption" from outside, an exteriority calling into question its sovereign point of departure in the aesthetics of existence. From the perspective of this specific discursive framework of a historical immanence after the death of God and the end of metaphysics, that interruption would point to another "death of God" – the death that the Trinitarian God Himself intended to die, in order to reveal, in the Son, the truth about the sovereign powers of this world as such. This other death of God signifies another end of metaphysics and another advent of God, as a liberation from the self's limitations in the human knowledge of ground, essence and structure – known as resurrection through love.

---

"A Preface to Transgression," where the practice of transgression is described as the result of the killing of God: "to kill God to liberate life from this existence that limits it" (Foucault 1977:32). For an excellent exposition of this central idea see Schmid 1991:146 ff.

4 The concept of "theo-drama" was introduced by Hans Urs von Balthasar in his *Theodramatik* (Balthasar 1973–1983). Theo-drama describes the intervention of God in the world as a dramatic one culminating in the death of God on the cross. *Theo-drama* is the middle work in von Balthasar's great theological Tryptichon, between his Christian *Theo-aesthetics* and his *Theo-logic*, thus moving from the aesthetic to the dramatic and then to the logic. All of these approaches are but explications of the trinitarian dynamics of God's essence. Cf. Schindler 2004 and Löser 2005.

(2) This omission in Foucault's account of antiquity corresponds to a no less surprising omission in his history of modern Parrhesia – that of Kierkegaard's name and his philosophical project,[5] which – by reconstructing Parrhesia for both the Socratic and the Christian way of life as specific modern options – initiated the first exodus from metaphysics, system and knowledge on the ground of an aesthetics of the individual and the singular self, to which Foucault himself subscribed.[6]

The answer to the question of why Foucault does not even mention Kierkegaard as the forefather of philosophy as a parrhesiastic technology seems to clarify the reason for the first omission as well. Foucault's aim ultimately is precisely the opposite of Kierkegaard's: He seeks to reduce the Christian way to the Socratic aesthetics of sovereign life and thereby replace and eliminate it. By this strategy, he not only rules out the possibility of an alternative Christian exodus from metaphysics; he also excludes the very possibility of a critique of his Nietzschean type of reverse theology or theo-aesthetics of the advent of the other god of sovereignty, transgression and potential dissolution in madness. Such a critique would point to the absolute limit of the discourse on Parrhesia, behind the game of limits and their transgressions, namely, the ontological difference between man and God and the potential pathologies emerging from the idea of an aesthetics of existence as permanent transgression.

Confronting Foucault's texts, we seem to stand before the empty grave of God, and we might ask ourselves why we are left only with an aesthetic critique of metaphysical knowledge and a theo-aesthetics that pushes life toward constant

---

5 As set out in *The Concept of Irony* (Kierkegaard 1965), *Either/or* (Kierkegaard 1959), *Philosophical Fragments / Johannes Climacus* (Kierkegaard 1985), *Concluding Unscientific Postscript to Philosophical Fragments* (Kierkegaard 1992) and *Practice in Christianity* (Kierkegaard 1991). In *The Point of View for My Work as an Author* (Kierkegaard 1962), Kierkegaard explains his strategy in terms of a parrhesiastic method of care for the truth of the self in need of therapy, developed not only against Hegelian metaphysics, but always as a coalition of the Socratic and the Christian ways of life. Of the numerous works on Kierkegaard see, e.g., Rudd 1997, Mooney 2007 and Hampson 2013.

6 The whole issue of the relationship between the Stoic and the Christian Parrhesia is dealt with in Foucault's *History of Sexuality*, especially Part 3, *The Care of the Self*. In the conclusion, Foucault writes: "One should not be misled by the analogy. Those moral systems will define other modalities of the relation to self: a characterization of the ethical substance based on finitude, the Fall and evil, a mode of subjection in the form of obedience to a general rule that is at the same time the will of God." (Foucault 1986:239) Foucault wants to secure positive Parrhesia against this religious form of obedience to the law and the rule of God. On the one hand, he is aware that the Stoic and the Christian ways of life are not so different in their growing ascetic approach, but, on the other, he rejects all submission to a fixed rule and a metaphysical-theological order.

transgression and overcoming of the self as a sign of the advent of another god, the god of power and transgression.

It is not in order to missionize Foucault or to perform a religious "hijacking" of his discourse that I wish to open a perspective on the Christian theo-drama as an alternative exodus from metaphysics. This point of departure ensues from Foucault's discourse itself, which is constantly moving toward the Christian conception of Parrhesia while simultaneously drawing away from it and ultimately replacing it by reducing it to a theo-aesthetics of permanent transgression. A critique of this strategy might thus well follow Kierkegaard's deconstruction of all metaphysics, aesthetics and theo-aesthetics from both perspectives, the Socratic and the Christian theo-dramas of truth, putting these discourses into a dialogical relationship with each other rather than reducing the one to the other on the basis of the sovereign subject. My critique will take the following form:

(1) As a first step, I shall briefly sketch Foucault's post-metaphysical strategies of comparison and separation between the Socratic and the Christian ways of life in antiquity and modernity, avoiding any definition of the human essence.

(2) I shall then turn to Foucault's last lecture. which deals for the first time with the New Testament itself, in order to discuss the significance of his omission of the Christological theo-drama.

(3) After a short analysis of Foucault's theology of aesthetic existence, I shall turn to the second omission, that of Kierkegaard's construction of the Socratic and Christian parrhesiastic ways of life as modern options. The purpose of this reading is to formulate a theological critique of Foucault's theo-aesthetics of power via the omitted theo-drama of truth, whose presence emerges in Foucault's account through the strategy of explicit omission.

## The Idea of a History of Philosophy as Parrhesia

Foucault's above-quoted summary on Parrhesia and philosophy can serve as an outline for his definition of the space and history of the subject, beyond its transcendental subjugation in an a priori essence, ground or origin. This exodus from any essence historicizes, contextualizes and situates subjectivity in its various existential, political and inter-subjective surroundings, in which it constantly constitutes and redefines itself on the basis of its own truth as a work of art.

It is not only the potential of this scene of truth to turn into a dangerous political game culminating in the tragedy of the parrhesiastic hero that reminds us of Nietzsche. The whole framework of this historical project of a reconstruction of Parrhesia as an art of life beyond any ideal essence presupposes a perspective beyond the Platonic/Christian framework of metaphysics. It presupposes the event of the "death of the Christian God," as an opening of the horizon to the possibility and transgression of a new self and, hence, to the possible advent of another, "positive" God of life. This interconnection between the death of God, the end of man and the transgression of any human essence as the scene of the appearance of the other gods is already developed in Foucault's earlier work:

> Rather than the death of God [...] what Nietzsche's thought heralds is the end of his murderer; it is the explosion of man's face in laughter, the return of the masks.[7]
> Is that not what Nietzsche was paving the way for when, in the interior space of his language, he killed man and God, both at the same time, and thereby promised with the return the multiple and re-illumined light of the gods?[8]

While Foucault's above-mentioned suggestion of an alternative history of philosophy explicitly excludes Christianity for modernity, he repeatedly compares the Socratic and Christian adoptions of Parrhesia in antiquity, not only in order to draw a sharp borderline between them, but also in order to point to analogies, similarities and approximations.[9] Thus, the border seems to move all the time, sometimes delineating a clear separation, but in the next example this limit will be transgressed and moved toward another differentiation and constellation. Like the modern artist, whom Foucault celebrates as possessing the sovereign power to transgress the limit at the moment it has been posited, the historian investigates the infinite facets and masks of a pragmatic subjectivity that will never obey any ready-made rule, general scheme or formula of its being. So the investigation of the antique Parrhesia and its relationship to Christianity is already governed by the post-metaphysical perspective on history and subjectivity.

It is of course impossible even to begin to demonstrate Foucault's art and mastership of the historian's game of drawing and transgressing the limits, but I believe one can still broadly distinguish three basic strategies here:

(1) For antiquity, it seems that Foucault – through his attention to similarities and differences – is pointing to a process of approximation between the Socratic and the Christian lifestyles, which he discusses mostly on the basis of the Greek Church Fathers.

---

**7** Foucault 1970:420.

**8** *Ibid.*:334.

**9** In the conclusion to *The Care of the Self* (Foucault 1986:235–240), Foucault quotes Zahn 1894 and Bonhoeffer 1911 as affirmations of his own attempt to demonstrate the analogies, while reminding the reader that the analogy is subverted by the Christian tendency to interpret human nature as sin and obedience to the law and rule of God.

(2) This process of approximation, culminating at the end of the last lecture in the Cynic's art of life, leads to a final removal of the limit to the Christian "technology" of Parrhesia itself. From now on, Foucault distinguishes, rather, between a good and a bad Christian pragmatics of an aesthetics of existence.

(3) The most significant limit is drawn between antiquity and modernity, since there is no mention in his lectures of a Christian alternative to the modern parrhesiastic art of existence. Foucault mentions the examples of Kant, Hölderlin and Nietzsche and of the modern artist in this context, without any reference to Christianity.

This last strategy becomes quite obvious in the case of the Cynic, which seems to be the true highlight of Foucault's account, since the Cynic no longer teaches a philosophy but rather lives this philosophy in his daily life; as it were, he "incarnates" the logos of philosophy in his concrete flesh. Foucault occasionally uses the concept of a "non-philosophy" for this kind of incarnated life.

While there seems to be hardly any difference between the Cynic's and the Christian way of life in antiquity – St. Jerome even recommends the example of Diogenes to his community – the Christian way of life disappears completely when Foucault adopts the Cynic as the perfect model for the modern aesthetics of life.

Here we can distinguish between two central interrelated issues: (1) the radical aesthetization of the parrhesiastic subject; and (2) the idea of the other god(s), corresponding to this aesthetic experience:

(1) Foucault presupposes a process of transformation between antiquity and modernity, a process of secularization whereby the cynical life of poverty and nakedness adopted by the Church Fathers is transmitted through the Franciscan brothers to the modern life forms of an aesthetic exception, culminating in the various cultural strategies of a modern aesthetic antinomianism.

> There is another reason why art has become the vehicle of Cynicism in the modern world. This is the idea that art itself, whether it is literature, painting, or music, must establish a relation to reality which is no longer one of ornamentation, or imitation, but one of laying bare, exposure, stripping, excavation, and violent reduction of existence to basics.[10]

This antinomianism articulates itself best in the radical modes of artistic transgression, culminating in the works of the artists that Foucault admires, from Baudelaire to Becket, from Hölderlin to Mallarme, Bataille or the music of Pierre Boulez, that is, in the art of breaking the rule in the moment it comes into play.

**10** Foucault 2011:188.

In its most radical form, this aesthetic transgression points to a dissolution of the self in madness, which Foucault celebrates in and with Hölderlin's poetry:

> Simultaneously, a zone is created, where language loses itself in its extreme limits, in a region where language is most unlike itself and where signs no longer communicate, that region of endurance without anguish: "Ein Zeichen sind wir, deutungslos" [We are a sign, uninterpreted]. The expansion of this final lyric expression is also the disclosure of madness.[11]

It is precisely this aesthetic experience of a permanent act of transgression of the rules and borders that Foucault regularly glorifies as the true consequence of the event of the death of God, in a radically new conception of human subjectivity being pushed beyond all known and accepted forms and figures to its utmost possibilities. Foucault finds this life of radical freedom and transgression realized in Pierre Boulez's music in a paradigmatic way, as a life of absolute presence, since the subject, "having destroyed all evidences and universals [...] constantly changes his place, never knows for sure what he will be or what he will think tomorrow, because his attention is absorbed totally by the *presence*."[12]

(2) Just when aesthetic secularization has overcome the Christian God in the event of the death of God, as the end of metaphysics, Foucault, like Nietzsche and Hölderlin, introduces the idea of the advent of the other gods, thus turning this secularization into a rather ambivalent event. Since philosophy, with Nietzsche, has recaptured the experience of the divine, it demands a non-positivist origin. This experience of the divine seems to be a metonym of the radical aesthetic life, which actualizes itself through the destruction and transgression of all rules, culminating in the total innovation of the self. The aesthetics of life is thus transformed from within the modern context into a kind of theo-aesthetics, indicating the fusion of the abstract conception of the self as a being beyond determination with its concrete forms, in a practice of destruction, transgression and innovation – that is, in the fusion of the human and the divine beyond the theological, beyond the Judeo-Christian infinite distance between Creator and creature.

**11** Foucault 1998a:17. Madness appears in Foucault's *Madness and Civilization* (Foucault 1988) as a "sovereign enterprise" always questioning the borders of reason. Together with Nietzsche, Nerval, Van Gogh and Artaud, Hölderlin is a "lightning flash" breaking through the borders of fixed rationality (*ibid.*:288).

**12** Foucault 2001b:138.

## Secularization between the Advent of the New God and Christian Theo-Politics

This tendency toward a quite ambivalent secularization – between the disappearance of God and the advent of the gods – not only determines the modern perspective of Foucault's alternative view on the history of philosophy; it also, as already suggested, affects and enhances the modes of description of the classical age. It is not only that life as an "origin without positivity," beyond any pre-stabilized metaphysical order, serves as Foucault's understanding of ancient subjectivity, which does not engage with Being, the realm of ideas, mathematics, the cosmic order or life after death. Socrates instead becomes the model of an existentialist politician and an artist of life, designed according to the Nietzschean model of an aesthetics establishing the freedom of the self by means of sovereign power beyond resentment. Even when Foucault mentions the gods in the ancient context, thus referring to a sphere of some kind of transcendence, these gods seem to be shaped according to the aesthetic art of life. They appear as models and representations of the mythical and aesthetic gods Nietzsche, affirming the idea of an eternal return, announced and predicted for the future, following the death of God.

This situation helps explain the evaluation that Foucault offers in differentiating between a good/positive and a bad/negative Christian way of life. While the good way rests on a kind of consensus and trust between the Parrhesiast and God, the bad one reflects the growing distance between the believer and his God and the appearance of such negative attitudes, created by God's rule and law, as guilt, regret, obedience and humility. "Where there is obedience there cannot be Parrhesia. We find again what I was just saying to you, namely, that the problem of obedience is at the heart of this reversal of the values of Parrhesia."[13] It is from this perspective that the approximation between the Cynic master of ascetic life and his Christian counterpart, presented by Foucault toward the end of his last lecture, becomes possible, presupposing the code of power and sovereignty as its fundament.

The Christian ascetic becomes a double of his sovereign Cynic counterpart precisely because his attitude is explained as perfect "self-domination"! Both are described as perfect masters of a sovereign will that is able to overcome the political sovereign powers because their will proves stronger.

The similarity between Epictetus's ideal Cynic martyr and the Christian martyr, however remarkable, becomes less surprising on the basis of this rather

**13** Foucault 2011:336.

hidden presupposition of a theo-aesthetics. Moreover, Foucault's perspective explains why the focus on the Christian martyr is developed primarily from the political – or more precisely, the politico-theological – perspective. In Epictetus's conception, as described by Foucault, the crowned sovereign becomes only a shadow of the Cynic ascetic sovereign and anti-king, who, by hiding his mission behind a façade of poverty, nakedness and public derision, rises to heaven and sits next to God.[14] It is at this point – in the very last chapter – that Foucault turns to the New Testament, to focus on the political theology of the apostle Paul, who, in confessing his truth before the powers, relies on his trust in God. Foucault describes the Christian martyr as the perfect model for the Parrhesiast as such.

> But in these New Testament texts, Parrhesia is also the sign of the courageous attitude of whoever preaches the Gospel. Here, Parrhesia is the apostolic virtue par excellence. And here we find again a meaning and use of the word which is fairly close to the Classical Greek or Hellenistic conception. Thus in the Acts of the Apostles, where the issue is Paul's vocation and the disciples', the apostles' initial mistrust of him. He is not taken to be a disciple of Christ. And then Barnabas recounts how he saw Paul at Damascus, and how he had seen him preach "frankly" in the name of Jesus: [...] He argued in this way with the Greeks and "they sought to take his life" [Acts of the Apostles 9:26–29].[15]

It is worth mentioning that Foucault refers in this context to the Catholic theologian Erik Peterson, who, in 1920, gave one of the first accounts of the history of the concept of Parrhesia and its transformations, from the Greek theater to the Stoics and Cynics and the Church Fathers.[16] In his lectures from these years, Peterson rescues Paul, whom he calls "the apostle of exception," from Nietzsche's denunciation of him as the Rabbi of resentment; turning this evaluation upside down, Peterson presents him as the martyr of a radical anti-imperial theo-politics.[17] Peterson based this theo-politics on the Christological event and turned it into a critical argument against Nietzsche and against Carl Schmitt's political

---

**14** *Ibid.*:274–275.

**15** *Ibid.*:330.

**16** See Foucault 2001a:178. The reference is to Erik Peterson's "Zur Bedeutungsgeschichte von Parrhesia" (Peterson 1929), which belongs to the period of Peterson's lectures on Paul as a theopolitician; see Peterson 1997. It was Barbara Nichtweiss (1992) who reintroduced this forgotten but central figure in modern theology to the intellectual public. On Peterson's impact upon current debates about political theology, his critique of Carl Schmitt and his relation to Giorgio Agamben, see Schmidt 2014.

**17** It was Nietzsche who rediscovered the politics of Paul; see Nietzsche 1980: §§42ff. According to Nietzsche, Paul's theology of the cross is not only a falsification of Christ's life practice but also a consequence of Jewish rabbinical resentment of Roman imperial power. Peterson (1997) reversed Nietzsche's position, giving Paul's politics a positive sense as the true Christian theology of sovereign power.[18] Foucault seems to have adopted Peterson's idea of a Christian theo-politics of the Parrhesiast Paul against the sovereign powers, but without its Christological fundament, thus re-integrating the Christian view into the framework of Nietzsche's anti-metaphysics of will, power and sovereignty!

We can summarize these primary observations as follows:

(1) The Nietzschean anti-metaphysics serves as the point of departure for Foucault's conception of an art of life, which can be re-projected onto ancient philosophy as "the daughter of Parrhesia" and the art of existence.

(2) The inception of philosophy is thus developed in a variety of parrhesiastic practices, culminating in the Socratic art of life and its transformations, which serve as the background to a comparison with the patristic adoptions of Parrhesia in Christian antiquity, leading to the demonstration of a process of approximation.

(3) While this analogy is valid for Antiquity, it is of no relevance to the Modern age, which favors the modern artist's model of the aesthetic life of exception and scandal. This move toward a modernity without Christianity strengthens the initial suspicion that Foucault's account of the ancient process of approximation between the Socratic and the Christian way of life is based on the Nietzschean assumption of a way of life of sovereign power and the return of the divine, which opened the space of Foucault's historical inquiry.

## The Missing Link: Christ's Theo-Drama of Truth

In his very last lecture, Foucault turns to the adoptions of the concept of Parrhesia in the Septuagint and the New Testament, thus relinquishing the patristic framework of the discussion in order to present the apostles Paul and John as perfect inheritors of the Greek concept. As indicated, the real surprise of this lecture, which proceeds on solid philological grounds, is that it does not mention the very messianic event itself, the Christological mystery of the revelation of God's Word or Truth in the Son's incarnation and death on the cross. This scene – referred to in the gospel of John as an act of parrhesiastic revelation of truth –

---

theopolitics against the sovereign imperial powers, which Peterson identifies with Schmitt's political theology.

**18** Peterson 1994 was a radical critique of the theological possibility of Schmitt's political theology, as set out in his *Politische Theologie* (Schmitt 1996). Schmitt would react to this critique much later, in *Politische Theologie*, II (Schmitt 1970). For a survey of this debate see Schmidt 2014.

constitutes the very fundament of all the Greek Christian practices of the Christian life, and it is the model for all Christian theo-politics.

Let us have a look at the scene in John 7. The chapter, which describes Jesus' retreat to Galilee before the Feast of Tabernacles, begins with the demand of his disciples to reveal himself by acting openly:

> After these things Jesus walked in Galilee, for he would not walk in Jewry, because the Jews sought to kill him. Now the Jews' feast of tabernacles was at hand. His brethren therefore said to him, Depart hence, and go into Judea, that thy disciples also may see the works that thou doest. For there is no man that doeth anything in secret, and he himself seeketh to be known openly. If thou do these things, shew thyself to the world. For neither did his brethren believe in him. Then Jesus said unto them. My time is not yet come; but your time is always ready. The world cannot hate you; but me it hateth, because I testify to it, that the works thereof are evil. (John 7:1–7)

The revelation of Christ as Messiah is supposed to occur as the culmination of an escalating series of events, following the accusations against Jesus as the Son of God and the seducer of the masses who have welcomed him as their Messiah. In this moment, the "Kairos" of Parrhesia, Christ will step out of his secrecy and reveal himself as the Truth about the powers of this world, and by his death he will "show plainly" the ultimate meaning of divine action as love and forgiveness for the sins of the powers:

> These things have I spoken unto you in proverbs: but the time cometh, when I shall no more speak unto you in proverbs, but I shall shew you plainly in the Father. (John 16:25)

This Parrhesia of Christ as the open proclamation of the meaning of the recondite proverbs that had preceded it not only reverses the political theology that derives sovereignty and power from God; it also reveals the truth about the power behind all power structures, political, social and personal, metaphysical or, rather, anti-metaphysical and aesthetic, in which the self finds itself captive or has captured itself. Christ not only reveals the truth, "He is the truth," since God himself, in this act of love, disposes of his own power and authority, in order to serve man and to testify to this truth with the "death of God" on the cross. This divine Parrhesia is thus grounded in the very act of "Kenosis," the evacuation of God by God himself, which Paul describes in his Epistle to the Philippians in the following famous dogmatic formula:

> Let this mind be in you, which was also in Christ Jesus: who, being in the form of God, thought it not robbery to be equal with God: but made himself of no reputation, and took upon him the form of a servant, and was made in the likeness of men. And being found in fashion as a man, he humbled himself and became obedient unto death, even the death of the cross. (Phil. 2: 5–8)

This is the Christological theo-drama of Truth, which is the foundation for all the analogies to the Socratic drama of truth. It illuminates the full contrast to be seen in this analogy, as it points always already to the Trinitarian mystery of Father, Son and Holy Spirit in the event of the death of God, which God himself chose, in order to liberate humankind from all its political, social, subjective and metaphysical forms of subjugation. This event indicates the end of metaphysics, celebrated by Nietzsche and Foucault, but from a theological perspective: God appears as the "Agapeic servant,"[19] the servant of love, who reminds humans that the source of all power lies in a misguided will and a misguided understanding of sovereignty and divinity. This is the power of transgression and the elimination of the absolute border separating the human and the divine, which the theologians call "sin" – the sin of rebellion against the absolute border between the human and the divine!

## The Second Omission: Kierkegaard as the Modern Parrhesiast

The first omission, in Antiquity, is of course connected to the second one, in the Modern age. Together, they function as the obverse of the two supposed appearances of Christ, the negative "Parousia," so to speak, that is such a present absence in Foucault's discourse. From the perspective of the second omission, it will be easier to explain the full meaning of the first.

(1) Like Foucault, Kierkegaard dismantled metaphysics, system and knowledge of the subject into an aesthetics of singular existence striving for freedom and truth. As with Foucault, this destruction aims at a liberation of subjectivity from its transcendental subjugation; it refers to the destruction and transgression of all finite forms, determinations and concepts in which subjectivity finds itself captive. For Kierkegaard, subjectivity aims at the restoration and actualization of freedom and possibilities in a concrete situation: "Every subject is an existing subject, and that fact must express itself in all the knowing, and in preventing the

19 See Desmond 2001. Desmond opposes Agape to Eros in a dialectical gesture, so that Eros and Agape are not mutually exclusive but rather complement each other in the process of selving. He thus reconciles what he calls "erotic sovereignty" with "agapeic service" and avoids the tendency to radical reductionism. In general, his philosophy understands itself as a "metaxology," a thinking in between the opposites, reconciling them through dialogue rather than dissolving them in a Hegelian *Aufhebung*, as an identity of differences. Desmond's thinking culminates in *God and the Between* (Desmond 2008), which accomplishes the move of the absolute from being and ethics to theology itself, rejecting the Hegelian God as realized identity and self-consciousness.

knowing arriving at an illusionary finality."[20] This specific negativity toward fixed forms in life is expressed in the individual's lifestyle and style of writing, so that Kierkegaard can say: "The only writer who really has style is the one who never has anything finished."[21]

(2) By this, Kierkegaard, like Foucault, performs a radical transformation from philosophy toward an aesthetics of existence, which can no longer reduce a human essence to universal predications, but rather turns to a narrative and dialogical language in which the self tries to give an account of its truth claims to itself and the other. In contrast to logic, this strategy is aesthetic, because it takes its point of departure from the sensual and concrete individual, which withdraws itself from all definition, system and norm. Philosophy, as in the case of Foucault, becomes a *non-philosophy*, turning polemically against "philosophy," which is captured in the illusion of knowledge and the identity of thought and being.

(3) It is precisely here that Kierkegaard's project, in its interpretation of this aesthetic orientation, differs from Foucault's, in at least two respects:

(a) Turning against Hegel's metaphysics and onto-theology – that is, the system of absolute being as self-knowledge, both in philosophy and in Christian dogma – Kierkegaard develops this existential and aesthetic move through the two ways of life, the Socratic and the Christian, without reducing one to the other. Instead, he holds them in tandem, simultaneously in coalition against the ready-made concept and in competition with each other. The Socratic way of life corresponds with emancipation from the philosophical concept, while the Christian way of life is a function of liberation from the conceptual fixation of Christian dogma in Hegel's system. The death of the metaphysical and onto-theological God thus becomes the symbol of the end of the captivity of both God and the human within the system of absolute Knowledge! Both ways of life represent a life of freedom that constitutes itself – in both cases – against all definitions as a loyalty to one's own truth, a truthfulness in light of openness toward possibility and the future. The self, as Kierkegaard formulates quite schematically on one occasion, becomes a synthesis of finite/infinite, of reality/possibility,[22] which in both cases situates itself in a concrete real and finite context but remains open to its possibilities, in order to resist system and definition and to confront every other with its truth.

---

**20** Kierkegaard 1992:68. Kierkegaard turns against Hegel and radically separates the system of logic from the art of life in existence: "Consequently there can be a logical system, but there can be no system for life itself" (*ibid.*:92). But God himself would of course be the system, not to be achieved by human thought.

**21** *Ibid.*:73.

**22** Kierkegaard 1954:146ff.

(b) But Kierkegaard not only turns against a metaphysics that closes itself in an absolute system as fulfilled reality; he also recognizes the ultimate danger of an absolute hypostasis of the idea of an aesthetic life as pure possibility.[23] Since the aesthetic phenomenon is situated beyond definition, there is a constant danger of misunderstanding this specific "being outside" the realm of thought as an attitude of absolute freedom from all determination. The move toward a radical destruction and transgression of life would potentially do the same thing as metaphysics: Rather than absolutize subjectivity in an absolute totality, it would absolutize the self in a compulsion for a permanent transgression of all boundaries and definitions, a supposed absolute infinity of subjectivity. From the perspective of the supposed synthesis of the self as reality/possibility, the metaphysical hypostasis turns "reality" and "determination" into absolutes, while the aesthetic hypostasis turns "possibility" and negation into absolutes, thus effectively imprisoning subjectivity in these modalities.

Aesthetic subjectivity, by potentially breaking through every border it has just created, dispenses with the possibility of retaining a continuity of the self, which, through these negations, splits up into disconnected fragments. Rejecting all determinations, it potentially denies all responsibility for its past and all possible forms of failure or guilt.

Kierkegaard's return to Parrhesia in both its Socratic and its Christian versions rejects this aesthetic path as another form of absolutist metaphysics. Unlike Foucault, he creates a dialogical equilibrium between the Socratic and the Christian truths and opposes it to the aesthetic absolute, the hypostasis of the aesthetic existence.

Kierkegaard is of course responding to the danger of an absolute aesthetics or theo-aesthetics of existence of the type that he identifies with the Romantic

---

**23** In the second part of *The Concept of Irony*, Kierkegaard analyzes the Romantic aesthetic consciousness, which will serve as the basis for his later diagnosis of aesthetic pathology. His basic point of departure is a total denial of all objectivity, by means of ironic transgression: "In irony the subject continually wants to get outside the object, and he achieves this by realizing every moment that the object has no reality" (Kierkegaard 1965:257). In "Balance between the Esthetic and the Ethical (Kierkegaard 1987), the judge, William, depicts the pathology of his friend the dandy as a "life of masquerade" (p. 153), in which the aesthetic subject lives in the illusion of being able to change his life every second, so that he wants now to be either a pastor or a lawyer, then to be a hairdresser or a bank teller, and in the end to be a critic, who can only affirm the basic vanity of all life (p. 166). The judge demonstrates the radical crisis of the aesthetic life by way of the example of the emperor Nero (pp. 184ff). This thought experiment presupposes that the aesthetic subject can really do whatever it wants, in order to show that this omnipotent self gets caught in its own inability to take any responsibility for anything, thus losing even the possibility of enjoying life.

idealists and ironists Tieck, Schlegel and Solger.[24] These Romantics translated Fichte's absolute idealism into an aesthetic way of life that, as the absolute ground of being, must be beyond all determination and thus must be defined as a Being of pure possibility and potentiality. From this metaphysical presupposition, they concluded that every concrete ego can only be a finite aspect and fragment of the Absolute, so that the self can never become fully "real" in a concrete form. The self is thus ironic at its base, presenting itself always in disguise, never revealing its true being, which could be uncovered only through an infinite transgression of all boundaries of definition. Of course, this act, thought through to its end, would lead to the dissolution of any concrete self, a notion that Foucault`s hero Hölderlin, whom Kierkegaard did not know, pushed to its ultimate poetic possibilities in madness. Romantic aesthetic subjectivity is thus always already on the way to becoming a "sign without meaning," revealing itself only through negations, and ultimately as madness.

According to Kierkegaard, neither this aesthetic negativity nor the converse metaphysical positivity are simply "given"; they must be understood as functions and movements of the concrete self, which is traumatized by its freedom and its finite conditions. Anxiety drives this self to try to escape itself and search for an ultimate and absolute life of power – either in the security of a present form, or in the permanent empowering of itself beyond any fixed form. Both absolutist movements thus turn out to be functions of a will to get beyond the concrete self: Instead of willing the concrete self – "as is," as an open synthesis of reality and possibility – the self wishes to absolutize itself against the potential weaknesses, dangers, anxieties and vulnerabilities of concrete life, either in an absolute reality and totality (metaphysics) or in an absolute possibility and infinity (aesthetics). While the metaphysical self is enclosed in a fixed form, the aesthetic self finds itself in a state of permanent transgression and escape from any enclosure. In either case, precisely because the self turns into a kind of God, captured in the fetters of its own will to power and absolute freedom, it ends up losing freedom and suffering despair.[25] Alongside a whole list of pathologies, the fundamental

---

**24** Cf. Kierkegaard 1965, especially part II.

**25** In "The Balance between the Esthetic and the Ethical" (Kierkegaard 1987), Kierkegaard describes the different stages of despair, up to the point where despair, in the figure of acedia, is revealed as sin. Nero, as the ultimate example of the aesthetic life, serves as the paradigm of this development. In *Sickness unto Death* (Kierkegaard 1954), Kierkegaard reconstructs this path in a systematic phenomenology of the different stages of despair, culminating in despair before God, which is the definition of Sin. Sin is taken not as a moral category, but rather as the effect of the self which refuses to become a concrete self, refusing to love itself and thereby refusing God's love.

despair generated by this captivity, which turns out to be the obverse side of the will to power, to absolute power, already indicates the need for another idea of the absolute, a transcendence beyond reach!

Kierkegaard seems to be both the ultimate model for a post-metaphysical philosophy of existential life – expressed in the dual path between the Socratic and the Christian options, relying on the singular aesthetic self – and the ultimate critic of any attempt to translate this aesthetic life into an absolute art of life and an existence of sovereign power. By rejecting the aesthetic life of sovereign power, Kierkegaard, radically unlike Foucault, opens the way for a nonreductive dialogue between the Socratic and the Christian ways of life.

## The Christian Theo-Drama of Love versus the Socratic Drama of Truth

According to Kierkegaard, the pathology of the self striving to escape its specific existential situation into an absolute form is the ultimate symptom of a fundamental neurosis and privation, namely, the self's incapacity to truly love itself. The self, striving to become absolute, obviously does not want to be a finite synthesis between reality and potentiality; it despises finitude, with its weakness, insecurities and anxieties. This means that the self fundamentally does not love itself. The movement toward the absolute reveals the self's basic failure to develop a positive relationship with itself, which delivers it, seeking to compensate itself for this lack, to the powers of power and, inescapably, to an agonistic immanence of despair. This is the birth of the self as the sovereign superman, idol or god, which is but the direct result of the sovereign will to "kill God." The self takes offense at the idea that God loves the individual self, because is cannot think of itself as loveable, and so it prefers to do away with the idea of God as love.[26]

Against Hegelian metaphysics and Romantic theo-aesthetics, with their transgression of the self toward the absolute, Kierkegaard develops his theo-psychology or therapy as a radical reversal of this logic and its specific direction. This leads to the idea of a countermovement as an evacuation of the self from all

26 Kierkegaard 1954:214–217. Here Kierkegaard tells the wonderful story of the poor laborer who is invited by the emperor to marry his daughter and cannot believe that this could ever happen. Kierkegaard's analysis of the story introduces the idea of an envy turned against oneself, which is grounded in the overwhelming effect of God's goodness, transcending human reason. Here he anticipates the phenomenological category of the saturated phenomenon, developed by Jean-Luc Marion; see, e.g., Marion 2001.

absolute forms and strategies, taking the self away from the absolute, to be actualized in the concrete self. This countermovement would have to be conceived as the radical interruption of the logic of the self's agonistic will to power. It would have to reveal the source of this power, the power driving the self beyond and against itself, capturing it in itself and delivering it to despair!

Kierkegaard finds this countermovement spelled out in the Christian theo-drama of truth – in God`s kenosis, his evacuation of himself as God and his incarnation in the figure of the "agapeic servant." The self-revelation of God in kenosis reveals the truth about power as a consequence of the deep lack of self-love. This is what the theologian Kierkegaard calls sin, which is not a moral category, but an attitude: the refusal of the self to enter into a love relation with itself, which would presuppose the love relation with God. Through this relationship, the self could open itself to a restoration of its lack, through reconciliation and forgiveness, reinstating its capacity to accept and receive love!

Kierkegaard introduces the theo-drama of kenosis as the event of the gift of love – against sin, which is nothing but the self's power to refuse love – in order to point to the limits of an aesthetic life and its potential theo-aesthetics. This event reveals the ultimate sin, inherent in any metaphysical or aesthetic absolutism, as the will to escape the self and compensate it with power for the lack of love.

The Christian theo-drama of truth not only reveals the fundamental problem of power and will, always already on the wrong aesthetic path toward the absolute as their "own," their "property"; it also calls into question the rather naïve Socratic assumption that the self will act according to its better understanding, as long as it has really understood what the right thing – truth – is. The Christian Parrhesiast is well aware that the will, despite having perfectly understood what the right thing is, will likely postpone, neglect, forget and possibly turn against its better understanding and do the opposite.

But Kierkegaard turns his skepticism against both the Christian and the Socratic Parrhesiast, since the Christian tends to forget his obligation to truth and sacrifice truthfulness to his understanding of the effects of sin, thus relying on an easy forgiveness; while the Socratic Parrhesiast tends to fall into despair about the enormous difficulty of being truly faithful to the understanding of truth. Since both ways of life are open to the future, both are in need of self-critique and constructive critique of each other. The Socratic and the Christian ways of life are not reducible, and the one cannot replace the other, since – according to Kierkegaard – they are simultaneously the two modes of a post-metaphysical Parrhesia detaching the subject from all pre-established forms and essences, and different forms of an awareness of the ways to truth and their possible failures!

## Dionysus against Christ

There are thus good reasons for Foucault's omissions, which can hardly be accidental, of the Christian theo-drama and of Kierkegaard's theo-psychology based on that event. They reflect Foucault's effort to reduce the Christian Parrhesia to the philosophical-Socratic way of life, and to replace it in the name of the self's presupposed sovereignty and will to power, to constitute itself. By pushing the border between the Socratic and the Christian Parrhesia, Foucault is always already concerned with the one and absolute border between the human and the divine, the basic ontological difference between human and divine being, which he seeks to overcome in his theo-aesthetics. Since this aesthetics of existence is based on a sovereign will to power that opens the space for another advent of the gods, Foucault's discourse is meant not to lead to a new openness to the Christian way of life, but rather to eliminate it without any regret or sense of guilt, by integrating it and reducing it to power and sovereignty. Submitting God to the powers of the sovereign self, Foucault's aesthetic art of life thus always already intends to abolish the very concept of sin.

Foucault seems to realize Nietzsche's prophecy of the advent of the superman as god, or of the god as superman. Where Nietzsche, in conceiving of himself as Dionysus crucified, was still torn by his vision of the other god, Dionysus, the true Antichrist, replacing Christ, Foucault seems to have accomplished this replacement through the idea of a practice and art of life, culminating in a theo-aesthetics "beyond sin" – beyond failure, guilt and regret. By actually replacing the Christian life – by ignoring the anti-metaphysical potential of the Trinitarian theo-drama – the Socratic drama of truth, especially the radical aesthetics of bare life and scandal represented and favored by the modern artist, is given over to the sovereignty and power of Truth without reconciliation.

Through its transformation, this drama of permanent transgression potentially leads to an absolute exhaustion of subjectivity, beyond its human limit! According to Foucault, it will be laughter, the Dionysian laughter of Nietzsche's mad man, that will liberate man from the burden of guilt for the death of God. It will liberate the murderer from the last traces of sin, made possible only by the murdered God: "Man will disappear. [...] Rather than the death of God [...] what Nietzsche's thinking heralds is the end of his murderer; it is the explosion of man's face in laughter, and the return of the masks; it is [...] the absolute dispersion of man."[27]

---

**27** Foucault 1970:460.

## References

Balthasar, Hans Urs von. 1973–1983. *Theodramatik*, I–IV. Einsiedeln: Johannes-Verlag.

Bonhoeffer, A. 1911. *Epiktet und das Neue Testament*. Giessen: Toepelmann.

Desmond, William. 2001. "The Community of Agapeic Service: The Intermediation of Transcendent Good." In: idem, *Ethics and the Between*. Albany: State University of New York Press. 483–515.

Desmond, William. 2008. *God and the Between*. Malden, MA: Blackwell.

Foucault, Michel. 1970. *The Order of Things: An Archaeology of the Human Sciences*. London: Tavistock.

Foucault, Michel. 1977. "A Preface to Transgression." In: idem, *Language, Counter-Memory, Practice: Selected Essays and Interviews*. Ithaca, NY: Cornell University Press.

Foucault, Michel. 1986. *The Care of the Self* (The History of Sexuality, 3; English transl. by Robert Hurley). New York: Pantheon.

Foucault, Michel. 1988. *Madness and Civilization: A History of Insanity in the Age of Reason*. New York: Vintage.

Foucault, Michel. 1998. *Aesthetics, Method and Epistemology* (English translation by Robert Hurley et al.), ed. James D. Faubion. New York: New Press.

Foucault, Michel. 1998a. "The Father's No. " In: Foucault 1998. 5–20.

Foucault, Michel. 1998b. "What Is an Author?" In: Foucault 1998. 205–222.

Foucault, Michel. 2001a. *Fearless Speech*, ed. Joseph Pearson. Los Angeles: Semiotext(e) (Distributed by MIT Press).

Foucault, Michel. 2001b. "Pierre Boulez oder die aufgerissene Wand." In: idem, *Short Cuts*. Frankfurt am Main: Zweitausendeins.

Foucault, Michel. 2005. *The Hermeneutics of the Subject: Lectures at the Collège de France, 1981–1982* (English transl. by Graham Burchell), ed. Frédéric Gros. New York: Picador.

Foucault, Michel. 2010. *The Government of Self and Others: Lectures at the College de France, 1982–1983* (English transl. by Graham Burchell). Basingstoke: Palgrave Macmillan.

Foucault, Michel. 2011. *The Courage of Truth: Lectures at the Collège de France, 1983–1984*, II (English transl. by Graham Burchell). Basingstoke–New York: Palgrave Macmillan.

Hampson, Margaret Daphne. 2013. *Kierkegaard: Exposition and Critique*. Oxford: Oxford University Press.

Kierkegaard, Søren. 1954. *Sickness unto Death*. Princeton, NJ: Princeton University Press.

Kierkegaard, Søren. 1959. *Either/Or* (English transl. by Alastair Hannay). Garden City, NY: Doubleday.

Kierkegaard, Søren. 1962. *The Point of View for My Work as an Author: A Report to History and Related Writings* (English transl. by Walter Lowrie and Benjamin Nelson). New York: Harper.

Kierkegaard, Søren. 1965. *The Concept of Irony, with Constant Reference to Socrates*, ed. Lee M. Capel. New York: Harper & Row.

Kierkegaard, Søren. 1985. *Philosophical Fragments / Johannes Climacus*. Princeton: Princeton University Press.

Kierkegaard, Søren. 1987. "The Balance between the Esthetic and the Ethical in the Development of the Personality." In: idem, *Either/Or*, II (English transl. by Howard V. Hong and Edna H. Hong). Princeton: Princeton University Press, 1987. 155–338.

Kierkegaard, Søren. 1991. *Practice in Christianity*, ed. Howard V. Hong and Edna H. Hong. Princeton: Princeton University Press.

Kierkegaard, Søren. 1992. *Concluding Unscientific Postscript to Philosophical Fragments*, ed. Howard V. Hong and Edna H. Hong. Princeton: Princeton University Press.

Löser, Werner. 2005. *Kleine Hinführung zu Hans Urs von Balthasar*. Freiburg im Breisgau–Basel–Vienna: Herder.

Marion, Jean-Luc. 2001. *De surcroît: Études sur les phénomènes saturés*. Paris: Presses universitaires de France.

Mooney, Edward F. 2007. *On Søren Kierkegaard: Dialogue, Polemics, Lost Intimacy, and Time*. Aldershot–Burlington, VT: Ashgate.

Nichtweiss, Barbara. 1992. *Erik Peterson: Neue Sicht auf Leben und Werk*. Freiburg im Breisgau: Herder.

Nietzsche, Friedrich Wilhelm. 1980. *Der Antichrist*. In: idem, *Sämtliche Werke: Kritische Studienausgabe in 15 Bänden*, ed. Giorgio Colli and Mazzino Montinari, VI. Munich–Berlin–New York: Deutscher Taschenbuch–De Gruyter.

Peterson, Erik. 1929. "Zur Bedeutungsgeschichte von parrhesia." In: W. Koepp (ed.), *Reinhold Seeberg Festschrift*, I: *Zur Theorie des Christentums*. Leipzig: Deichert. 283–297.

Peterson, Erik. 1994. "Monotheismus als politisches Problem." In: idem, *Theologische Traktate*, ed. Barbara Nichtweiss. Würzburg: Echter.

Peterson, Erik. 1997. *Der Brief an die Römer*, ed. Barbara Nichtweiss and Ferdinand Hahn. In: idem, *Ausgewählte Schriften*, VI. Würzburg: Echter.

Rudd, Anthony. 1997. *Kierkegaard and the Limits of the Ethical*. Oxford: Clarendon Press.

Schindler, D.C. 2004. *Hans Urs von Balthasar and the Dramatic Structure of Truth: A Philosophical Investigation*. New York: Fordham University Press.

Schmid, Wilhelm. 1991. *Auf der Suche nach einer neuen Lebenskunst: Die Frage nach dem Grund und die Neubegründung der Ethik bei Foucault*, I. Frankfurt: Surhkamp.

Schmidt, Christoph. 2014. "The Return of the Katechon: Giorgio Agamben contra Erik Peterson." *Journal of Religion*, 94/2. 182–203.

Schmitt, Carl. 1996. *Politische Theologie: Vier Kapitel zur Lehre von der Souveränität*, 7th edition. Berlin: Duncker & Humblot.

Schmitt, Carl. 1970. *Politische Theologie*, II: *Die Legende von der Erledigung jeder politischen Theologie*. Berlin: Duncker & Humblot.

Zahn, T. von. 1894. *Der Stoiker Epiktet und sein Verhältnis zum Christentum*. Erlangen: E.T. Jacob.

# Contributors to This Volume

**Rivka Feldhay**
Cohn Institute for History and Philosophy of Science and Ideas, Tel Aviv University, and Minerva Humanities Center, Tel Aviv University

**Yohanan Friedmann**
Institute of Asian and African Studies, The Hebrew University of Jerusalem, and Department of Middle Eastern and Islamic Studies, Shalem College, Jerusalem

**Jonathan Garb**
Department of Jewish Thought, The Hebrew University of Jerusalem

**Simon Gerber**
Berlin-Brandenburgische Akademie der Wissenschaften

**Israel Gershoni**
Department of Middle Eastern and African History, Tel Aviv University

**Christoph Markschies**
Berlin-Brandenburgische Akademie der Wissenschaften

**Paul Mendes-Flohr**
The Van Leer Jerusalem Institute

**Christoph Schmidt**
Department for German Language and Literature, The Hebrew University of Jerusalem

**Johannes Zachhuber**
Faculty of Theology and Religion, University of Oxford

# Index

## Places and Institutions


Action Francaise 27
Africa 88, 91, 92
Albertina University VII
al-Azhar University 81
al-Mansura (school) 81
Arabian Peninsula 83, 93
Asia 88, 91
Athens 71

Balkans 90
Barqayn, village 81
Bourbon monarchy 23, 24, 89
Brunswick, Duchy of 4, 6

Cairo 80, 81, 84
Caribbean colonies 66
Catholic Church 21
Collegio dei Nobili, Parma 60
Collegio Romano 58
Colonial British Egyptian Ministry of Justice 81

Damascus 81, 122
Daqahiliyya, province of 81

East Prussia VII
Egypt 79–110
England 88
Erets Israel 35
Europe VIII, 12, 35, 37–39, 41, 49–61, 65, 80, 88, 89, 100–102, 108

Florence 56
France 27, 28, 66, 88, 92
Franciscans 119

Galilee 124
Gnadau 8

Halle (university of) 4, 6
Hamburg 7
Helmstedt (university of) 4
Hijaz 81, 83
Hijaz railway 81
Ḥizb al-Umma – see Party of the Nation
Al-Ḥizb al-Waṭanī – see Nationalist Party

Immanuel Kant Baltic Federal University VII
Israel, state of 43, 44
Italy 39
Izbica 42

Jaffa 81
Jehovah's Witnesses 8
Jena (university of) 6
Jerusalem 71
Jesuits 49, 50, 56, 57, 60, 61

Kaliningrad VII, VIII
Kaliningrad, cathedral of VII
Khedivial Secondary School 81
Khedivial School of Law 81, 84
Kingdom of God 1, 17, 72
Königsberg VII
Köthen 8

Lichtfreunde (Friends of the Light) VII, 8
Lutheran Church 6

Mecca 81, 82
Medici Court 56
Medina 79, 81–83
Middle East 80, 88
Moab 37
Mormons 8
Mount Sinai 36, 39

Nationalist Party (Al-Ḥizb al-Waṭanī) 86, 87, 92, 93, 102 n. 67
New Apostolic Church 8
New York VIII, 43
Nile Valley 84, 85, 90

Ottoman Empire 92


https://doi.org/10.1515/9783110723984-009

Padua 40
Palestine 81
Parma 58, 60
Party of the Nation (Ḥizb al-Umma) 80
Pentecostalism 8
Pisa (university of) 55
Poland 68
Pope, papacy 20, 49, 51, 58
Prague VIII, 35, 37
Promised Land 75
Prussia VII, VIII, 6, 15, 16
Prussian State of the Teutonic Order VII

Rome 21, 27, 57, 58
Russia, Russian Empire VII, 11

Sachsen-Weimar-Eisenach, Duchy of 7
Safed 34, 35, 37, 39, 42
Sweden 57
Syria 93

Tabūk 81
Third Reich 75
Turkey 80, 83, 93

Ukraine 11
United Kingdom 12

Venice 58
Verein für Wissenschaft der Juden 65

Weimar Republic VIII
West Germany 75 n. 49

## Names

'Abbās Ḥilmī II, Khedive 86, 94
'Abd al-Ḥamīd II, Sultan 92
'Abduh, Muḥammad 97, 98, 109
Abraham 40
Abulafia, Abraham 33
Adham, Ibrahim Pasha 81
Adorno, Theodor 72
Agnon, Shmuel Joseph 67 n. 15
Albert, Duke of Prussia VII
Al-Fārābī 107
Amīn, Qāsim 95, 105, 106
Antichrist 131
Archimedes 57
Arendt, Hannah 66
Aristotle 94, 105–107
Armenteros, Carolina 25
Artaud, Antonin 120 n. 11
Asad, Talal 109
Augustine of Hippo 13, 14, 28–30

Baal Shem Tov, Israel 42
Bacharach, Naftali 38, 39, 44
Balthasar, Hans Urs von 115
Barnabas 122
Barth, Karl 5
Baudelaire, Charles 67 n. 15, 119
Bauman, Zgymunt 69, 70
Becket, Samuel 119
Bell, Daniel 76
ben 'Attar, Ḥayyim 44
Benjamin, Walter VIII, 67–69, 71–74, 76
Bodin, Jean 52, 53, 60
Bonald, Louis de 18, 21–26, 28
Boulez, Pierre 119, 120
Bruno, Giordano 50
Buber, Martin VIII, 67, 71, 72, 74–76

Casati, Paolo, SJ 57, 58, 60
Christ – see Jesus Christ
Christina, Queen of Sweden 57
Church Fathers 4, 115, 118, 119, 122
Clavius, Christoph, SJ 49
Comte, Auguste 12, 24–28
Condorcet, Marquis de 56
Copernicus, Nicholas 49
Cordovero, Moses 35, 37
Cromer, Lord 90, 91
Cynics 119, 121, 122

David 38
Descartes, René 54, 56, 79, 114
Desmond, William 125 n. 19
Diderot, Denis 56, 97
Diogenes 119
Dionysus 131
Dreyfus, Alfred 27
Durkheim, Émile 12, 24, 25 n. 46, 27–30, 51

Eisenstadt, Shmuel VIII, 51
Epictetus 121, 122

Fanon, Franz 66
Farīd, Muḥammad 87
Farnese family 60
Fontenelle, Bernard Le Bovier de 56
Foucault, Michel IX, 113–131
Frederick the Great, King 15, 16
Frederick William III, king of Prussia 6

Galilei, Galileo 50, 54–57
Gesenius, Wilhelm 6
Ghali, Butrus 102 n. 67
Giddens, Anthony 25
Goethe, Johann Wolfgang von 7
Goeze, Melchior 7
Gogh, Vincent van 120 n. 11
Gorst, Eldon 99
Gregory XIII, Pope 49
Gregory, Brad 12
Guldin, Paulus, SJ 57

Hallamish, Moshe 33
Hase, Karl August 6–8
Hegel, Georg Friedrich Wilhelm 5, 6, 74, 126
Heidegger, Martin 74
R. Ḥelbo 35
Helvétius, Claude Adrien 56, 97
Henke, Konrad 4, 6
Hitler, Adolf 75
Hobbes, Thomas 15, 22, 24, 73

Hofman, Amos 97
d'Holbach, Baron 97
Hölderlin, Friedrich 115, 119, 120, 128
Horkheimer, Max 72
Horowitz, Isaiah 37, 38, 40, 44
Hourani, Albert 96
Hume, David 79
Hundt-Radowsky, Hartwig von 66 n. 9
Hütter, Leonhard (Hutterus) 6

Ibn Bāja 107
Ibn Rushd 107
Ibn Sīnā 107
Idel, Moshe 33

Jāwīsh, ʿAbd al-ʿAzīz 87
Jerome, St. 119
Jesus Christ 2, 5, 8, 17, 23, 113, 122–125, 131
John, Apostle 115, 123

Kafka, Franz 67–69
Kāmil, Muṣṭafā 87, 92
Kant, Immanuel VII, 1–4, 65, 79, 97, 106, 110, 114, 119
Kepler, Johannes 54, 56
Kierkegaard, Søren 113, 116, 117, 125–131
Kollwitz, Käthe VII
Kook, Abraham Isaac Hakohen 43, 44

Lamennais, Félicité de 18
Laplace, Pierre-Simon 56
Leibniz, Gottfried Wilhelm 79
Leiner, Mordecai Joseph 42, 43
Lessing, Gotthold Ephraim 7
Lilith 38 n. 25
Locke, John 15, 79, 94, 96
Loew, Judah (Maharal) 35–37, 44
Luria, Isaac 35, 37
Luṭfī al-Sayyid, Abū ʿAlī 79–82
Luṭfī al-Sayyid, Aḥmad IX, 79–110
Luther, Martin 8, 49, 50
Luzzatto, Moses Ḥayyim 40, 44

Macherey, Pierre 25
Magid, Shaul 34, 43
Maistre, Joseph de 12, 18–23, 26
Mallarme, Stephane 119
Marheineke, Philipp 5
Marin, Louis 59
Marion, Jean Luc 129 n. 26
Marx, Karl 51, 72
Mary, Virgin 26
Maurras, Charles 27
Mersenne, Marin 56, 57
Messiah 38 n. 25, 39, 69, 72, 124
Milbank, John 25
Mill, John Stuart 94
Montesquieu 88, 89, 94, 96
Moses Ḥayyim Ephraim of Sudylkow 42
Mosse, George 44
Muḥammad 79, 82, 103
Muratori, Ludovico Antonio 56

R. Naḥman of Bratslav 41–44
Nerval, Gerard de 120 n. 11
Newton, Isaac 25, 54, 58
Nichtweiss, Barbara 122 n. 16
Nietzsche, Friedrich 114, 115, 117–123, 125, 131
Nisbet, Robert 25
Novalis 12

Paul, Apostle 38, 115, 122–124
Peter, St. 21
Peterson, Erik 122, 123
Po, river 58

Rahab 40
Reno, river 58
Röhr, Johann Friedrich 6, 7
Rose, Gillian 67
Roth, Philip 43
Rousseau, Jean-Jacques 12, 15, 17, 18, 21, 22, 24, 26, 28, 29, 94, 96
Rupp, Friedrich Julius Leopold VII
Ruth 37, 38

Saint-Simon, Henri de 25, 26
Schachter-Shalomi, Zalman 43
Schelling, Friedrich Wilhelm Joseph 3, 5–7
Schilling, Heinz VIII
Schlegel, Friedrich 128
Schleiermacher, Friedrich 3–6
Schmitt, Carl 15, 122, 123 n. 18

Scholem, Gershom 67–69, 72
Simmel, Georg 70, 71
Sinai, Mount 39
Slezkine, Yuri 64
Smith, Wilfred Cantwell 52
Socrates 121
Solger, Karl Wilhelm Ferdinand 128
Sorotzkin, David 36
Spaemann, Robert 23, 25
Spencer, Herbert 94
Spinoza, Baruch 15
Stoics 122
Strauss, Leo 71–74, 76

Tau, Tsvi Israel 44
Tieck, Ludwig 128
Tolstoy, Leo 108
Torricelli, Evangelista 56
Turgot, Anne Robert Jacques 56

Valle, Moshe David 40, 41, 44
Varro, Marcus Terentius 13–15, 29, 30
Veblen, Thorstein 70
Vico, Giambattista 56
Volta, Alessandro 56
Voltaire 56, 89, 97

al-Wardānī, Ibrāhīm Nāṣif 102 n. 67
Weber, Max 51
Wegscheider, Julius 4–7
Wijnhoven, Jochanan 34
Wolfson, Elliot 33–35, 44

Zunz, Leopold 65

www.ingramcontent.com/pod-product-compliance
Lightning Source LLC
Chambersburg PA
CBHW032229080426
42735CB00008B/779